Writing with Clarity and Style

A Guide to Rhetorical Devices for Contemporary Writers

Robert A. Harris

Pyrczak Publishing

P.O. Box 39731 • Los Angeles, CA 90039

Although the author and publisher have made every effort to ensure the accuracy and completeness of information contained in this book, we assume no responsibility for errors, inaccuracies, omissions, or any inconsistency herein. Any slights of people, places, or organizations are unintentional.

Project Director: Monica Lopez.

Cover design by Robert Kibler and Larry Nichols.

Editorial assistance provided by Sharon Young, Brenda Koplin, Cheryl Alcorn, Randall R. Bruce, and Erica Simmons.

Set in Palatino 11/15 (body) and 10/15 (examples), and CG Omega 11/15 (exercises and tables). Headings in CG Omega.

Printed in the United States of America.

ISBN 1-884585-48-5

Contents

Introduction   vii

Chapter 1: Balance   1
  1.1 Parallelism   1
  1.2 Chiasmus   5
  1.3 Antithesis   7
  Style Check 1: Rhythm   9

Chapter 2: Emphasis I   11
  2.1 Climax   11
  2.2 Asyndeton   12
  2.3 Polysyndeton   14
  2.4 Expletive   15
  Style Check 2: Demetrius on Beginning and Ending Stress   18

Chapter 3: Emphasis II   21
  3.1 Irony   21
  3.2 Understatement   22
  3.3 Litotes   24
  3.4 Hyperbole   26
  Style Check 3: Emphatic Positioning   27

Chapter 4: Transition   29
  4.1 Metabasis   29
  4.2 Procatalepsis   30
  4.3 Hypophora   33
  Style Check 4: Transitions of Logic   35

Chapter 5: Clarity   39
  5.1 Distinctio   39
  5.2 Exemplum   41
  5.3 Amplification   42
  5.4 Metanoia   43
  Style Check 5: Clear versus Opaque Writing   45

Chapter 6: Figurative Language I   47
  6.1 Simile   47
  6.2 Analogy   52
  6.3 Metaphor   54
  6.4 Catachresis   58
  Style Check 6: Demetrius on Metaphor   59

Chapter 7: Figurative Language II   63
  7.1 Metonymy   63
  7.2 Synecdoche   65
  7.3 Personification   68
  Style Check 7: Freshness   71

Chapter 8: Figurative Language III   73
  8.1 Allusion   73
  8.2 Eponym   75
  8.3 Apostrophe   76
  8.4 Transferred Epithet   78
  Style Check 8: Persona   80

Chapter 9: Syntax I   83
  9.1 Zeugma   83
  9.2 Diazeugma   84
  9.3 Prozeugma   85
  9.4 Mesozeugma   86
  9.5 Hypozeugma   87
  9.6 Syllepsis   88
  Style Check 9: Cumulative and Periodic Sentences   89

Chapter 10: Syntax II   93
  10.1 Hyperbaton   93
  10.2 Anastrophe   94
  10.3 Appositive   96
  10.4 Parenthesis   98
  Style Check 10: Parataxis and Hypotaxis   99

Chapter 11: Restatement I   103
  11.1 Anaphora   103
  11.2 Epistrophe   105
  11.3 Symploce   107
  Style Check 11: Demetrius on Short Sentences for Emphasis 108

Chapter 12: Restatement II   111
  12.1 Anadiplosis   111
  12.2 Conduplicatio   112
  12.3 Epanalepsis   114
  Style Check 12: Style   115

Chapter 13: Restatement III 119

13.1 Diacope 119

13.2 Epizeuxis 120

13.3 Antimetabole 122

13.4 Scesis Onomaton 123

Style Check 13: Demetrius on Increasing Vividness 124

Chapter 14: Sound 127

14.1 Alliteration 127

14.2 Onomatopoeia 130

14.3 Assonance 133

14.4 Consonance 134

Style Check 14: Texture 136

Chapter 15: Drama 139

15.1 Rhetorical Question 139

15.2 Aporia 141

15.3 Apophasis 143

15.4 Anacoluthon 144

Style Check 15: The Levels of Style 146

Chapter 16: Word Play 149

16.1 Oxymoron 149

16.2 Pun 151

16.3 Anthimeria 154

Style Check 16: Tone 156

Appendix A: Rhetoric in Context I—Newspaper Editorial 159

Appendix B: Rhetoric in Context II—Business Memorandum 163

Appendix C: Rhetoric in Context III—Social Worker's Report About a Client 167

Appendix D: Rhetoric in Context IV—Graduate School Application Essay 171

Appendix E: Rhetoric in Context V—Short Story 175

Appendix F: Winston Churchill—A Speaker's Rhetoric 179

Index 183

Alphabetical Contents

Alliteration	127		Expletive	15
Allusion	73		Hyperbaton	93
Amplification	42		Hyperbole	26
Anacoluthon	144		Hypophora	33
Anadiplosis	111		Hypozeugma	87
Analogy	52		Irony	21
Anaphora	103		Litotes	24
Anastrophe	94		Mesozeugma	86
Anthimeria	154		Metabasis	29
Antimetabole	122		Metanoia	43
Antithesis	7		Metaphor	54
Apophasis	143		Metonymy	63
Aporia	141		Onomatopoeia	130
Apostrophe	76		Oxymoron	149
Appositive	96		Parallelism	1
Assonance	133		Parenthesis	98
Asyndeton	12		Personification	68
Catachresis	58		Polysyndeton	14
Chiasmus	5		Procatalepsis	30
Climax	11		Prozeugma	85
Conduplicatio	112		Pun	151
Consonance	134		Rhetorical Question	139
Diacope	119		Scesis Onomaton	123
Diazeugma	84		Simile	47
Distinctio	39		Syllepsis	88
Epanalepsis	114		Symploce	107
Epistrophe	105		Synecdoche	65
Epizeuxis	120		Transferred Epithet	78
Eponym	75		Understatement	22
Exemplum	41		Zeugma	83

Introduction

The purpose of this book is to provide you with a set of practical tools for making your writing clear, interesting, and effective. Whatever your subject or audience, appropriate use of the devices presented in this book will give your writing the life, freshness, and texture that will make it appealing.

As I write this Introduction, I am sitting in a bookstore, surrounded by perhaps 10,000 books. Some of these books are waiting to be snatched up by eager readers. Others are waiting until they are called to become egg cartons. The difference is admittedly determined in part by each book's subject matter and the publisher's marketing expertise, but at least some of the difference is determined by writing style. Better written books are better selling books.

You may not be planning to write a book. However, the same thinking applies to any written product. Faced with billions of words written every day in our information-glutted age, readers are forced to make choices about what to read and how carefully to read it. Today, if you want your writing to be read, you must have more than just good ideas. If you want your writing to be read, it must be clear and interesting.

The philosophy behind this book is straightforward:

♦ **The purpose of writing is to communicate.** Clear, smooth writing communicates better than muddy, awkward writing. Well-organized sentences with carefully placed emphasis make writing more easily accessible to readers.

♦ **Interesting writing is more likely to be read than boring writing.** Every kind of writing, for every audience, can be made more interesting. Fresh expressions, visually appealing language, even an occasional dramatic effect or play on words—all of these will help maintain a reader's interest.

♦ **Skillful rhetoric is a friend, not a foe, of clarity and effectiveness.** The rhetorical devices in this book are presented as a set of practical tools for enhancing communication. Well used, rhetoric will help you to become a better writer.

Therefore, please put aside any prejudice you have toward the word *rhetoric*. This is not a book to help politicians construct bombastic harangues; it is not a book to help *artistes* create flowery emptiness. This is a book for students and professionals who wish to add power, liveliness, and interest to their writing. This is a book that teaches rhetoric as the art of using language effectively.

The Method.

The book is designed to teach by showing contemporary examples rather than solely by description. Study the several usage examples for each device to see how they can be applied. Follow up by completing the exercises to gain additional familiarity and to give yourself practice. If you keep a personal journal or have a journal assigned for a course, practice the devices there as well.

Whichever devices you employ in your assigned writing will depend on the subject and audience. Not every device may be suitable for every essay, research paper, legal brief, feature article, or software manual; but every kind of writing can benefit from the addition of structure, color, rhythm, and texture that these devices make possible.

The Names and Terms.

Many of the devices described in this book have names that may sound odd to a modern reader. Do not be put off by them. These names (coming from Greek and Latin) provide a quick and handy method of identification—call it the jargon of rhetoric, if you will—making the discussion much easier than having to describe the nature or effect of a device each time it is mentioned. The pronunciation guides for each term generally follow the regular dictionary method, except for two substitutions. In place of the reduced vowel sound that appears as an upside-down e in many dictionaries, I have used *uh* or *u*. In place of dieresis-*a* (*ä*) to represent the *a*-sound in a word like *father*, I have used *ah*. I hope these minor adjustments will make the pronunciations transparent.

Organization of the Book.

Organizing what is to some extent a miscellaneous collection of tropes, figures, and schemes (here they are all called *devices*) was accomplished first by grouping devices of similar structure or effect and then by arranging the groups in the order of building blocks. For example, parallelism is presented first because many other devices make use of it.

The devices themselves often have several uses and effects, so that putting them into groups in chapters labeled Emphasis or Clarity was partly a matter of creating convenient chunks for study. Other groupings would have been equally good. Thus, for example, even though a particular device is not listed in Chapter 2 on Emphasis, the device may still be largely useful for emphasizing an idea. In the same way, many devices are useful for enhancing clarity even though only some of them are in Chapter 5 under the title of Clarity.

Acknowledgments.

Thanks to Fred Pyrczak, acquisition editor and publisher, for his help defining this book and suggesting many improvements. Thanks to Clay Austin for his careful reading of the manuscript. Thanks to Jennica Brune for her help testing the exercises. Special thanks to my wife, Rita, for allowing me the release time to write this book. Last, as well as least, I'd like to thank my two Chihuahua baby dogs, Wolf and Bear, for their semi-reliable companionship during many hours at the keyboard, and for inspiring at least one example for the book.

Chapter 1
Balance

The most important goal of writing is to be clear
without being boring. —Aristotle, *Poetics*

Writing well involves more than merely putting one word after another. Good writing has structure and balance that make it easy to read and understand. This chapter covers a few of the basic techniques for creating more balanced and therefore more readable prose. As with the other devices in the book, these can be learned and appreciated best if you read the examples aloud to get a feel for the effect. When you work on the exercises, read your own sentences aloud and listen to them carefully. Writing is aural (there is sound in silent reading) as well as visual.

1.1 Parallelism.

Parallelism (PAR uh lel iz um) is the presentation of several ideas of equal importance by putting each of them into the same kind of grammatical structure. Each of the ideas is ordered or phrased similarly:

> **Example 1.1.1**
> <u>To think carefully</u> and <u>to write precisely</u> are interrelated goals.

The sentence in this example contains two subjects, developed in the same grammatical style (two infinitives, *to think* and *to write;* each with an adverb, *carefully* and *precisely*). Thus, *to think carefully* is paralleled with *to write precisely*. Compare that sentence to the following example, which presents the same ideas but which does not contain parallelism:

> **Example 1.1.2**
> To think carefully and precise writing are interrelated goals.

If you study these two sentences, you will notice that parallelism provides several benefits:

- ◆ **Clarity.** Sentences with parallelism are easier to understand than those without it because a repeated grammatical structure requires less mental processing than a series of new structures.
- ◆ **Balance.** Parallel structures make it easier for the reader to hold each of the ideas in mind while reading the subsequent ideas.

- ♦ **Rhythm.** Most readers hear in their minds the words they read. The sound, the musical nature, of the words adds to (or detracts from) the overall reading experience. Parallel structures are more rhythmic than nonparallel structures.
- ♦ **Elegance.** Another way to describe elegant writing might be to say *interesting writing.* Appropriate use of parallelism provides a texture—even a beauty—to writing that makes it more readable and engaging.

Parallelism is one of the building blocks for many of the other devices in this book. It is so important for clarity that breaking parallelism is usually considered a writing fault. In fact, *revise for parallelism* is a common notation in the margins of student essays. Compare the following sentences.

> **Example 1.1.3**
> *Parallelism broken:* Julie liked reading the paper more than lunch.
> *Revised for parallelism:* Julie liked reading the paper more than eating lunch.

> **Example 1.1.4**
> *Parallelism broken:* The mechanic applied extra force to the bolt so that it would seat properly and he wanted it to be sufficiently tight.
> *Revised for parallelism:* The mechanic applied extra force to the bolt so that it would seat properly and tighten sufficiently.

In Example 1.1.3 above, confusion may arise from the broken parallelism because the sentence sets up an unbalanced contrast between *reading the paper* and *lunch.* What about lunch is being compared? Going to lunch, eating lunch, relaxing during lunch? In Example 1.1.4, the revision more clearly shows that proper seating and proper tightening are parallel reasons (both following the *so that*) for the mechanic's actions.

Any sentence parts can be paralleled, any number of times, with the usual number being two, three, or four. Following are several examples of the various elements that can be paralleled.

> **Example 1.1.5**
> *Parallel subjects:* <u>The carefully trimmed trees in the front yard</u> and <u>the spectacularly clean patio in the back</u> revealed the meticulous nature of the homeowner.

> **Example 1.1.6**
> *Parallel verbs and adverbs:* The agency had <u>frequently received</u> but <u>seldom revealed</u> a large number of crank phone calls.

> **Example 1.1.7**
> *Parallel objects:* The doctor carefully examined <u>the heel,</u> <u>the ankle,</u> and <u>the toes.</u>

Example 1.1.8

Parallel verbs and objects: Mom went to Judy's room and <u>gave her a drink</u>, <u>pulled up her blanket</u>, and <u>kissed her forehead</u>.

Example 1.1.9

Parallel prepositional phrases: The dropped apple floated <u>down the river</u> and <u>under the bridge</u>.

Note that effective parallelism does not require that every element match exactly, as the following example shows.

Example 1.1.10

Rough parallelism: <u>After the concept drawings for the building are completed</u>, but <u>before we submit them to the planning department</u>, the design committee will take one more look at them.

Exact parallelism: <u>After the concept drawings for the building are completed</u>, but <u>before the planning review in city hall is started</u>, the design committee will take one more look.

One definition of parallelism is "recurrent structural similarity," and as the word *similarity* implies, there is some latitude. Note also that paralleling rather long subordinate clauses helps the reader hold the entire sentence more easily and clearly in mind.

Example 1.1.11

These early critics—<u>who point out the beauties of style and ideas</u>, <u>who discover the faults of false constructions</u>, and <u>who discuss the application of the rules</u>—usually produce a much richer understanding of the writer's essay.

(In the example above, the second and third use of *who* is optional and will still be implied if omitted. See the discussion of the zeugmatic devices in Chapter 9 for further information about implying words in various constructions.)

Parallelism is often useful for expressing contrasts or alternatives (see antithesis, Section 1.3 in this chapter).

Example 1.1.12

<u>Baking in the summer sun</u> and <u>rusting from the winter rains</u>, the tractor deteriorated a little more each year.

Example 1.1.13

Flying a plane is more complicated than <u>turning a few knobs</u> and <u>pulling a few levers</u>.

In practice, various sentence elements are combined into parallel structures that form either a piece of a sentence, an entire sentence, or even more than one sentence. Following are some examples of these possibilities.

Example 1.1.14

Parallelism for emphasis at the end of a sentence: I shall never envy the honors which wit and learning obtain in any other cause, if I can be numbered among the writers who have given <u>ardor to virtue</u> and <u>confidence to truth</u>.
—Samuel Johnson

Example 1.1.15

Parallelism of an entire sentence: The goal of a theoretical science is truth, but the goal of a practical science is performance. —Aristotle

Example 1.1.16

Parallelism of two sentences: After the first test, which used the rubber seal, the cylinder showed a ten-centimeter stain on the underside. After the second test, which used the new neoprene seal, the cylinder was completely unblemished underneath.

Exercise 1.1.1

Underline the parallel structures in the following sentences.
Example: The Fenns drove <u>through the meadow</u> and <u>into the forest</u> before setting up camp.

(a) To install new carpeting, workers must first remove the old carpet, prepare the surface, and then lay down the matting.
(b) Next, the installers need a sharp knife and a sturdy straightedge to cut the new carpet along carefully measured lines.
(c) Several workers are often needed to haul the carpet into the house, up the stairs, and across the room.

Exercise 1.1.2

Write a sentence imitating the model sentence below, using parallelism where the model does.
Example model: He liked to eat chocolate donuts and drink strong coffee.
Example imitation: She wanted to hear the spring concert and buy the new CD.

Model sentence: The old books and the wrinkled maps remained on the tables, gathering dust and turning yellow.

Exercise 1.1.3

Write a sentence containing parallel elements for each item below, according to the instructions.

      (a) Use parallel verbs and adverbs, as in Example 1.1.6.

      (b) Include parallel elements at the end, as in Examples 1.1.9 and 1.1.13.

      (c) Use parallel phrases, as in Examples 1.1.12 and 1.1.14.

1.2 Chiasmus.

Chiasmus (kī AZ mus) is a type of parallelism (where similar elements of a sentence are balanced with each other) in which the balanced elements are presented in reverse order rather than in the same order. Chiasmus is useful for creating a different style of balance from that offered by regular parallelism. Where parallelism balances elements in the same order (A, B is balanced by A, B), chiasmus reverses the order (A, B is balanced by B, A).

Example 1.2.1

                      verb   *adverb*   *verb*   *adverb*

Parallelism: The code breakers worked constantly but succeeded rarely.

                      verb   *adverb*   *adverb*   *verb*

Chiasmus: The code breakers worked constantly but rarely succeeded.

Chiasmus is effective for bringing two elements close together for contrast or emphasis, as you can see with the adverbs *constantly* and *rarely* in the example above. The chiastic structure places them almost next to each other for greater contrast than would be provided by a strictly parallel structure.

    Another useful effect of chiasmus results from the natural emphasis given to the end of a sentence. Note in the example below how the word *forgotten* receives greater stress when it appears as the last word of the sentence.

Example 1.2.2

Parallelism: What is learned unwillingly is forgotten gladly.

Chiasmus: What is learned unwillingly is gladly forgotten.

In addition to contrast and emphasis, chiasmus can add beauty to sentences with no sacrifice of clarity. Reversing the order of independent and subordinate clauses is one way to do this.

Example 1.2.3

Parallelism: When the house was finished, the buyers moved in; but when the insects invaded, the buyers quickly moved out again.

Chiasmus: When the house was finished, the buyers moved in; but they quickly moved out again when the insects invaded.

In the example above, the chiasmus also prevents a pronoun reference problem. In the parallel form, suppose the writer had said, "When the house was finished, the buyers moved in; but when the insects invaded, they quickly moved out again." In such a case, *they* would create an unclear reference because it could refer either to *buyers* or to *insects*. Thus, in the parallel example, the words *the buyers* must be repeated to avoid confusion. Note how elegantly the chiasmus permits a clear use of *they*.

Notice in the following example how the writer uses both parallelism (the first two clauses parallel each other, as do the last two) and chiasmus (the first half of the sentence is in chiastic balance with the last half of the sentence) to explain why he loves books:

Example 1.2.4

If you come to them, they are not asleep; if you ask and inquire of them, they do not withdraw themselves; they do not chide if you make mistakes; they do not laugh at you if you are ignorant. —Richard de Bury

The reversal of the balance from parallelism also allows you to alter the emphasis within the sentences. If a strictly parallel construction would place the emphasis on the wrong idea, rearranging the order might be the remedy, as in Example 1.2.5 below.

Example 1.2.5

Parallelism: The prime minister smiled at the audience when he was introduced. However, he frowned after the cameras were turned off.

Chiasmus: The prime minister smiled at the audience when he was introduced. However, after the cameras were turned off, he frowned.

Here, chiastic structure puts the emphasis on *frowned* rather than *turned off*. Note, however, that rearranging parallel sentences is not always effective. In Example 1.2.6 below, the sentence using chiasmus emphasizes the relatively unimportant *sorting* at the end.

Example 1.2.6

Parallelism: Walking through the junkyard, the inventors spoke excitedly of their plans for a flying boat. Later on, sorting through the selected materials, they showed more reserve about the possibilities.

Chiasmus: Walking through the junkyard, the inventors spoke excitedly of their plans for a flying boat. They showed more reserve about the possibilities later on while sorting through the selected materials.

When you craft your sentences using parallelism, experiment with a chiastic arrangement also. Examine the varying effects resulting from moving elements around.

Exercise 1.2.1
Revise each of the following sentences from parallel to chiastic form. Pay attention to the difference in effect created by each. Which version seems more effective in each case?
  (a) After startup, always check the pressure readings, but every hour check the voltage level.
  (b) With wood you get easier cutting and nailing, but with steel you avoid termites.

Exercise 1.2.2
Revise each of the following sentences from chiastic to parallel form. Pay attention to the difference in effect created by each. Which version seems more effective in each case?
  (a) If the peaches are ripe, turn on the canner. Turn on the cider press if the apples are ripe.
  (b) The buckle should be fitted securely and regularly adjusted.

1.3 Antithesis.

Antithesis (an TITH uh sis) contrasts two ideas by placing them next to each other, almost always in a parallel structure. You may have noticed in reading about parallelism and chiasmus above that those structures lend themselves easily to setting up contrasts. Developing contrasts is important for clear writing because a powerful way to clarify an idea is to show how it differs from another idea. (You may have read the advice about creating good explanations: First, say what something is like; then say what it is not like.)

By using a parallel structure for presenting a contrast, antithesis produces clarity, balance, and emphasis, all of which contribute to memorability.

Example 1.3.1
To err is human; to forgive, divine. —Alexander Pope

Example 1.3.2
That's one small step for man, one giant leap for mankind. —Neil Armstrong

Antithesis can convey a sense of complexity by presenting opposite or nearly opposite truths. By placing these contrasting ideas in the same grammatical position in the sentences using parallelism (Section 1.1, above), the contrast is more emphatically pointed out to the reader.

Example 1.3.3

Success makes us proud; failure makes us wise.

Example 1.3.4

If we try, we might succeed; if we do not try, we cannot succeed.

Note in the example above how *might* and *cannot* are naturally contrasted and emphasized by the structure of the sentence. Compare that with the same idea in a sentence without antithesis:

Example 1.3.5

We might succeed if we try; but if we do not try, then I do not think we can succeed.

Antithesis is also useful for making distinctions or for clarifying differences between ideas. Notice the contrast between legality and morality in the next example.

Example 1.3.6

I agree that is it legal; but my question was, is it moral?

Here the difference between legality and morality is called to the reader's attention by the parallel positioning of the contrasting words.

Usually, antithesis is recommended because of its power of emphasis, but it also makes understanding easier for the reader. As mentioned under the discussion of parallelism above, the parallel structure makes the sentence easier to decode. Adding an antithetical structure to the parallel structure makes the contrast easier to see and remember.

Exercise 1.3.1

Rewrite each of the following sentences into a sentence using antithesis to contrast the ideas. Feel free to omit any wordiness that interferes with the emphasis.

Example sentence: We made this area into a little park, and the fact that we removed a parking lot to do it seems not to be the thing to focus on.

Example revision: In this area, we created a park even though we destroyed a parking lot.

(a) When we jumped out of the airplane, Amy said the feeling of free falling was thrilling; I was terrified, though.
(b) This proposal calls for a thick retaining wall, but a wall that is strong should be a part of the proposal also.

Exercise 1.3.2

Write sentences of your own that contain antithetical constructions, as follows.

(a) Contrast single words, as in Example 1.3.6.

(b) Contrast phrases rather than just single words, as in Example 1.3.3.

Style Check 1: Rhythm.

Even though most prose does not have a regular or poetic meter, prose does still have a rhythm, created by the collection of stressed and unstressed syllables in all the words. Most readers subvocalize (that is, they hear the sound of the sentences in their minds) so that attention to the sound and rhythm of your writing is important, even though you are not writing a speech. A good check is to read your writing aloud—or better, have someone else read it aloud. Is the language balanced and smooth, flowing easily? Or is it jerky and awkward, clattering along? Practice moving a word here or there, writing a better phrase, or revising for parallel elements. Remember that improving rhythm is not "prettifying"; it is adding ease of understanding and even enjoyment to your thoughts.

Review Questions.

1. Determine whether each sentence contains straight parallelism or chiasmus. Write in *P* or *C* as appropriate.

   _____ The engine of the cruise ship was peacefully quiet; the plumbing was almost deafeningly loud.

   _____ To catch him on the phone required twenty phone calls, but an act of Congress would be needed to see him in person.

   _____ Across the river they could see their offices, while under the trees together they could feel their hearts.

   _____ When you speak, they will listen. They will act when you lead.

2. "The Broken Window theory tells us that, in order to reduce crime, arresting criminals is important, but painting over graffiti is crucial." This sentence contains
   A. parallelism only.
   B. antithesis only.
   C. parallelism and antithesis.
   D. neither parallelism nor antithesis.

3. Which one of the following does **not** contain antithesis?
   A. She laughed while he fumed.
   B. What we already have is reason; what we need now is imagination.
   C. She cried and I cried.

4. Which elements in this sentence are parallel? "To determine a reasonably profitable and competitively low price for a meal, some restaurants multiply the food cost of an item times four and charge that."
   A. *to determine* and *restaurants multiply*
   B. *reasonably profitable* and *competitively low*
   C. *food cost* and *an item*
   D. none of the above

Chapter 2
Emphasis I

The ablest writer is a gardener first, and then a
cook. His tasks are, carefully to select and culti-
vate the strongest and most nutritive thoughts,
and, when they are ripe, to dress them whole-
somely, and so that they may have a relish.
—J. C. and A. W. Hare

Not every idea a writer presents is as important as every other idea. Many ideas serve to support the key ideas being developed. Effective writing, then, helps the reader distinguish between the more and the less important ideas by emphasizing the more important ones. Many of the devices in this book are suitable for creating emphasis because they call attention to words or ideas by the structure of presentation. (You saw an example of this with antithesis in the previous chapter.) The devices in this chapter and the next are especially useful for emphasis.

2.1 Climax.

Climax (KLĪ maks) is the presentation of ideas (in words, clauses, sentences, etc.) in the order of increasing importance. At the level of an entire essay, climactic order is commonly used for arranging the points presented to produce the effect of increasing strength and emphasis. This same feeling of turning up the volume works at the sentence level also. Compare these lists, where the items increase in importance:

Example 2.1.1
Random order: When the bucket fell off the ladder, the paint splashed onto the small rug, the drop cloth, the Rembrandt painting, and the sofa.
Climactic order: When the bucket fell off the ladder, the paint splashed onto the drop cloth, the small rug, the sofa, and the Rembrandt painting.

Example 2.1.2
Random order: Before buying the house, inspect the carpet for wear, the foundation for cracks, the roof for leaks, the plumbing for rusty water, and the paint for chipping.
Climactic order: Before buying the house, inspect the paint for chipping, the carpet for wear, the plumbing for rusty water, the roof for leaks, and the foundation for cracks.

As Example 2.1.2 above demonstrates, climax produces a logically natural sense to the presentation of ideas as well as the sense of increasing emphasis—in other words, a gradation. (The Latin term for climax is *gradatio*, the root of *gradation*.) On the other hand, the randomly ordered list appears to have no sense to its arrangement, but directs the reader's attention randomly. Climax, then, is another strategy for adding clarity.

Exercise 2.1.1

Rewrite the following sentences, rearranging the elements in the lists into climactic order.

(a) Today we enjoy many benefits of modern technology, including life-saving antibiotics, ballpoint pens, and refrigerators.

(b) Natural water storage includes the oceans, ponds, lakes, and puddles.

2.2 Asyndeton.

Asyndeton (uh SIN duh tahn) consists of omitting conjunctions between words, phrases, or clauses in a list. A list of items without conjunctions gives the effect of unpremeditated multiplicity, of a spontaneous rather than a labored account.

Example 2.2.1
When he returned, he received medals, honors, riches, titles, fame.

The lack of the conjunction *and* between the last two elements in the list gives the impression that the list is not only spontaneous but perhaps incomplete. Compare the difference here:

Example 2.2.2
With conjunction: The fruit market displayed apples, peaches, pears, and nectarines.
Asyndeton: The fruit market displayed apples, peaches, pears, nectarines.

Example 2.2.3
With conjunction: The moist, rich, and fertile soil yielded willingly to the plow.
Asyndeton: The moist, rich, fertile soil yielded willingly to the plow.

When the items in a list are arranged in climactic order (discussed in the previous section), asyndeton can be particularly effective and more emphatic than if a conjunction were used between the last two items. Compare the difference:

Example 2.2.4

With conjunction: The investigator spent the day in the ruins wondering, searching, thinking, and understanding.

Asyndeton: The investigator spent the day in the ruins wondering, searching, thinking, understanding.

With single nouns or short phrases, omitting the conjunctions can create the effect of multiple appositives (see Chapter 10, Section 10.3), as if the writer is presenting synonyms rather than several different descriptions. Compare these:

Example 2.2.5

Conjunction: She was a winner and a hero.

Asyndeton: She was a winner, a hero.

Example 2.2.6

Conjunction: The dog was old, but it was his loyal friend, his constant companion, and his eager helper.

Asyndeton: The dog was old, but it was his loyal friend, his constant companion, his eager helper.

Asyndeton, climactic: The dog was old, but it was his eager helper, his constant companion, his loyal friend.

Note the subtle but elegant effect in the second asyndeton of Example 2.2.6, using climactic order. The sense seems to be that the writer is not just stringing out a descriptive list, but struggling mentally for just the right term to describe his dog. In the process, the reader benefits from the sense of reaching up to ever more significant terms while also seeing each of the other terms used during the writer's thought process. Contrast this with the example using the conjunction, where the three terms appear to be little more than a list of complimentary terms.

Almost any sentence elements normally connected by commas can be presented asyndetically. The key is to assure that the sentence is clear. For example, you would probably not want to write, "Jane, Tom went to the store" because the reader might understand the sentence to be a comment to Jane about Tom's whereabouts, rather than the statement that the two went to the store together.

Used to present entire clauses, asyndeton takes on a more subtle flavor, especially when used in connection with balance or parallelism or another device such as anaphora (see Chapter 11, Section 11.1), which this example demonstrates:

Example 2.2.7

In books I find the dead as if they were alive; in books I foresee things to come; in books warlike affairs are set forth; from books come forth the laws of peace. —Richard de Bury

Exercise 2.2.1

Convert the following sentences to asyndeton.

   (a) The fireworks lit the sky with red and blue and green and white and yellow.

   (b) Around the light they saw moths, beetles, mosquitoes, and gnats.

Exercise 2.2.2

For each item below, write a sentence using asyndeton, according to the instructions.

   (a) Use a string of three or more words for the elements, as in Example 2.2.1.

   (b) Use a string of three phrases for the elements, as in Example 2.2.6.

2.3 Polysyndeton.

Polysyndeton (pol ē SIN duh tahn) is the use of a conjunction between each word, phrase, or clause and is thus structurally the opposite of asyndeton. The rhetorical effect is different as well. While asyndeton usually creates the feeling of a spontaneous, even hurried enumeration or an enumeration where one term seems to replace another, polysyndeton produces the feeling of a deliberate piling up, a one-added-to-another multiplicity.

Example 2.3.1

They read and studied and wrote and drilled. I laughed and played and talked and flunked.

Example 2.3.2

Asyndeton: Within six hours, the computer virus had spread worldwide, infecting mail servers, Web servers, home users, business networks.

Polysyndeton: Within six hours, the computer virus had spread worldwide, infecting mail servers and Web servers and home users and business networks.

The multiple conjunctions in polysyndeton call attention to themselves and therefore add the effect of persistence or intensity or emphasis to the other effect of multiplicity. The repeated use of *and* stresses the sense of piling up; repeated use of *or* emphasizes alternatives; repeated use of *nor* stresses qualifications.

Example 2.3.3

And to set forth the right standard, and to train according to it, and to help forward all students towards it according to their various capacities, this I conceive to be the business of a university. —John Henry Newman

Example 2.3.4

They had neither power, nor influence, nor money, nor authority; but they told a simple and persuasive tale that soon reached Congress.

Example 2.3.5

Everyone who owns a house, whether of brick or wood or plaster or mud, says to the world, "This is my realm, my castle."

Exercise 2.3.1

For each sentence below, copy the sentence. Then rewrite the sentence, first using asyndeton, then using polysyndeton. Finally, write *Best* in parentheses by the version you think is the most effective.
   (a) The sparkle of clean water, the peace of silent skies, and the inspiration of giant trees—all these attract me to the forest.
   (b) In that nation, the farmers often have no rakes, hoes, shovels, or pitchforks.
   (c) Before beginning the questions, ask the group members how they feel, offer them beverages, and ask if they are comfortable.

Exercise 2.3.2

Rewrite your sentences from Exercise 2.2.2 on page 14, using polysyndeton. Use a different set of conjunctions (such as *and* for the first sentence and *or* for the second). For each sentence, explain whether asyndeton or polysyndeton is more effective.

2.4 Expletive.

You may be familiar with the word *expletive* (EKS pluh tiv) in reference to words not suitable for good company: Obscenities are, indeed, sometimes referred to as expletives. However, there are many expletives quite appropriate for use in good writing.

An expletive is a word or short phrase, often interrupting a sentence, used to lend emphasis to the words immediately before and after the expletive. The forced pause created by the expletive, together with the expletive itself, brings focus and emphasis to that part of the sentence. Compare the sentences below:

Example 2.4.1

Without expletive: The lake was not drained before April.
With expletive: The lake was not, in fact, drained before April.

Notice that there is a natural tendency to emphasize the *not* and the *drained* on each side of the pause in order to keep the continuity of the thought.

Expletives are often placed near the beginning of a sentence, where important information has been placed. (The beginning of a sentence is the second most emphatic position, with the end being the most emphatic.)

Example 2.4.2
The evidence is, indeed, plentiful, but it is not self-interpreting.

Because expletive words and phrases are recognized as emphasizers, they can be placed at the very beginning of a short sentence in order to signal that the entire sentence is unusually important.

Example 2.4.3
Clearly, the engineers now had several new options.

Example 2.4.4
In short, there are no extra funds to distribute.

When the sentence is abruptly short, the expletive can be placed at the end rather than the beginning. When the expletive follows a noun or verb in a short sentence, the whole sentence is emphasized. When the expletive follows a modifier (adjective or adverb), the modifier receives most of the emphasis.

Example 2.4.5
Expletive following a noun: It was a difficult excavation indeed.
Expletive following a modifier: The excavation was difficult indeed.

An expletive can emphasize both the words near it in the sentence and a phrase attached to it for quite a striking effect:

Example 2.4.6
The Bradys, clearly overwhelmed by the publicity, fled from the press attention and the new friends who wanted a share of the lottery winnings.

As mentioned earlier, the forced pause created when the expletive interrupts the sentence generates much of the emphasis. For this reason, any kind of interruption in a sentence can cause the words around it to be emphasized. Thus, transitional words and adverbs, among others, can be used for emphasis. Notice the difference in rhythm, speed, and emphasis in the following pairs.

Example 2.4.7
Without interruption: Many of the customers demanded a refund.
With interruption: Many of the customers, however, demanded a refund.

Example 2.4.8

Without interruption: "Your last remark contradicted itself," he noted.

With interruption: "Your last remark," he noted, "contradicted itself."

The table below lists many of the more commonly used expletives. When you decide that the emphasis of an expletive is desirable, try out several of these to find the best fit with your subject and sentence structure. Some will work better than others; some may be awkward in the given context.

Expletives		
after all	for all that	in short
anyway	generally	in sum
as I said	I hope	incidentally
assuredly	I suppose	indeed
at least	I think	it seems
by the way	importantly	naturally
certainly	in any event	of course
clearly	in brief	on the whole
decidedly	in fact	remarkably
definitely	in general	to be sure
emphatically	in other words	without a doubt

A final word of encouragement and caution is needed. Expletives can be powerful and effective tools of emphasis, and their variety can permit substantial creativity in their use. Experiment and analyze to find just the right usage. As with any device, though, be careful not to overuse this one. You may have heard the proverb, "Where everything is important, nothing is important." Similarly, if you use an expletive to emphasize one or two sentences in every paragraph, your writing will appear overblown and, perhaps, ridiculous.

Exercise 2.4.1

Add an appropriate expletive to each of these sentences, placing it where it will be most effective. What, in each sentence, needs emphasis most? As you select an expletive in each case, try several and notice the different meanings they give to the sentences.

(a) These early treatments of the disease were crude, but they formed the first steps toward modern control of infection.

(b) These three plums are still edible.

(c) Expletives are useful writing tools, but should not be overused.

Exercise 2.4.2

Rewrite each of the following sentences, moving the expletive to a more effective position. State in a sentence why the new position is preferable.

    (a) Indeed the food was cold, but we ate it anyway.

    (b) You could search the Web and hope to find something there, of course.

    (c) In fact, this was the result of chaos in the newsroom.

Style Check 2: Demetrius on Beginning and Ending Stress.

According to the classical Greek writer Demetrius in his book *On Style*, when you wish to write an emphatic sentence, the first and last syllable of the sentence should be long or stressed. If the sentence has more than one clause, then the first syllable of each clause should also be stressed.

Style Check Example 2.1

Weak: Until we know more, we cannot proceed properly.
Stress: un TIL we know MORE, we CAN NOT pro CEED PROP er ly.

Strong: Nothing can be done until we know more.
Stress: NOTH ing can be DONE un TIL we KNOW MORE.

Note in this example that the word *until* consists of an unstressed syllable (*un*) followed by a stressed syllable (*TIL*). Similarly, *properly* consists of a stressed syllable (*PROP*) followed by two unstressed syllables (*er*) and (*ly*). Thus, both the beginning and the ending of this sentence are unstressed, and to Demetrius, unemphatic. In the second sentence, the word *nothing* consists of a stressed syllable (*NOTH*) followed by an unstressed syllable (*ing*). Similarly, the last two syllables of the sentence, KNOW and MORE, are both stressed. The second sentence, then, is more effective because of these emphases. Compare the following pairs of sentences for a better understanding.

Style Check Example 2.2

Weak: Across the land the rain has grown heavier.
Stress: a CROSS the LAND the RAIN has grown HEAV i er.

Strong: Everywhere the heaviness of the rain has increased.
Stress: EVE ry where the HEAV i ness of the RAIN has in CREASED.

Style Check Example 2.3

Weak: An important part of forceful writing is the rhythm of it.
Stress: an im POR tant PART of FORCE ful WRIT ing is the RHYTH m of it.

Strong: Emphasis in writing by stressing the right words is an important skill.
Stress: EM pha sis in WRIT ing by STRESS ing the RIGHT WORDS is an im POR tant SKILL.

If you understand this lesson from Demetrius, you will now also understand why the title of this book is *Writing with Clarity and Style* instead of *A Guide to Writing with Style and Clarity.*

Review Questions.

1. Which sentence shows the most effective climactic order?
   A. Last month the clinic treated 44 cuts and bruises, 3 sprains, and 116 colds or flu.
   B. Last month the clinic treated 3 sprains, 44 cuts and bruises, and 116 colds or flu.
   C. Last month the clinic treated 116 colds or flu, 44 cuts and bruises, and 3 sprains.

2. Determine whether each sentence contains asyndeton or polysyndeton. If the sentence contains asyndeton, mark A in the blank; if it contains polysyndeton, mark P; if it contains neither asyndeton nor polysyndeton, mark N.
   _____ All a writer needs is a pad, a pen, and a place to think.
   _____ Semiotics includes the study of nonverbal communication, where a message is discerned in the gum on the sidewalk or the feel of a knob or the wink of an eye.
   _____ The engineers for the bridge traced the lines of force from the roadbed to the suspension cables to the vertical supports to the foundation.
   _____ Everywhere they looked in the cave produced more excitement: They saw stalactites, stalagmites, crystal pools, transparent fish, blind beetles, hanging bats.

3. Add an appropriate expletive to each of the following sentences.
   (a) He did not take the position lightly. He was present at every meeting.
   (b) The new coating should extend the corrosion resistance of the pipe by a year.
   (c) We can expect an increase in attendance at the convention this year.

4. Which sentence provides the beginning and ending stress recommended by Demetrius in Style Check 2?
   A. The reports existed in writing but everyone ignored them.
   B. Existing written reports were ignored by everyone.
   C. Written reports existed but were universally ignored.

Notes

Chapter 3
Emphasis II

A timely touch of the sublime blasts everything
else away—like the strike of a bolt of lightning—
and reveals the writer's true power in a flash.
—Longinus, *On the Sublime*

This chapter provides you with several more devices for creating emphasis in your writing. Used with care and art, these devices will call attention to your subject rather than to themselves. As always, the test is effectiveness in the particular application of the device: Try out several versions of the idea you want to express, and keep the best.

3.1 Irony.

Irony (Ī ruh nē) involves a statement whose hidden meaning is different from its surface or apparent meaning. Often, the ironic or implied meaning is the opposite of the literal meaning.

> **Example 3.1.1**
> When the tow truck driver pulled up, he saw the girl sitting in the rain on the spare tire, her prom dress ripped, grease on her face, mud on her shoes. As he stepped out of the truck, she asked him, "Does this mean my fun is over?"

The context of her remarks tells us that the girl is experiencing an ordeal, not having fun, so her question comes across as ironic. Notice that a feeling of humor is often attached to ironic statements because both irony and humor often share a sense of unexpected incongruity.

Another form of irony occurs when a statement reflects the opposite of what the reader might reasonably expect under the circumstances. An old joke is perhaps the most effective clarification:

> **Example 3.1.2**
> "The food here is terrible," said Jane, "and the portions are so small."

In this example, complaining about the size of the portions is ironic (that is, the opposite of what is expected) because we do not expect anyone to want larger servings of terrible food. Similarly, irony is created when a conclusion opposite of our expectations is reached, as in the following example.

Example 3.1.3

The bill was hastily and thoughtlessly written, filled with loopholes, and probably unconstitutional; so, of course, it passed on the first vote.

The bill's passing is ironic because we do not expect bad legislation to pass easily.

Irony often serves as an effective device of emphasis because of the surprise it generates. The reader receives a mental processing shock when the logic or conclusion of the sentence differs from expectation. As a result, the point is made more forcefully than it would have been had the thought ended as expected.

The first rule of effective irony is that your readers must clearly understand it as irony. Satirists who use irony usually include some indication that they are doing so or rely on the clearly ridiculous nature of the situation to alert the reader. Nevertheless, they are often misunderstood. (Jonathan Swift is still denounced by literal readers of *A Modest Proposal*, furious because they believe he is actually proposing cannibalism.) Take some care, then, that the context of your ironic statements clearly reveals their nature.

Sarcasm, by the way, involves an irony that is critically contemptuous. For example, if someone dives into a pool with a belly flop, a sarcastic remark would be, "That was certainly Olympic quality."

Exercise 3.1.1

For each sentence below, state whether or not the sentence is ironic. If so, state why.

   (a) Johnny, I have told you a million times: Don't exaggerate. People will stop taking you seriously.
   (b) The investor pulled his money from the stock market and invested in precious stones.
   (c) I'm sorry, ladies and gentlemen, but the speech on "The Importance of Punctuality" will be delayed half an hour because our speaker has not arrived yet.

3.2 Understatement.

Understatement deliberately expresses an idea as less important than it actually is. The degree, significance, or quantity involved is reduced (usually substantially), either for the purpose of ironic emphasis or for the sake of politeness. A common application is to emphasize something that already involves an extreme situation. Taking something that is already extreme and attempting to exaggerate it for emphasis would not be effective, so the opposite approach is taken. For example, suppose parents wish to caution their children to drive carefully and not to stay out too late. They could not effectively use exaggeration to describe the grief they would feel if something went wrong, so they understate it, as the following example shows.

Example 3.2.1

You know, we would be a little disappointed if you were to be hit by a drunk driver at 2:00 A.M., so we hope you will come home early.

Here, the understatement conveys the point emphatically by contrast with the true feelings rather than by exaggerating them.

Because of the contrast between the actual situation and the understated expression of it, understatement usually involves an ironic effect, adding a feeling of wit or even humor.

Example 3.2.2

As the pilot stood there in his singed and slightly bloodied shirt, he looked over the wreckage of the airplane he had just crawled out of and said, "Well, that sure shook the boredom off my day."

Understatement also serves as a tool for modesty and tactfulness. When you present your arguments in a persuasive essay, understating the effect you claim for them will help you avoid the charge of egotism on one hand and unwarranted conclusions on the other. Readers are always more pleased to discover that the force of an argument is stronger, rather than weaker, than the writer claims. As Samuel Johnson put it, "It is more pleasing to see smoke brightening into flame, than flame sinking into smoke." By understating your conclusions, you allow your reader to decide more favorably toward your argument. If you overstate your claim, your reader may feel that you are trying to push him or her into a conclusion that does not follow. Compare the following:

Example 3.2.3

Not understated: The second law of thermodynamics proves conclusively that this theory is utterly false and ridiculous.

Understated: The second law of thermodynamics suggests that this theory is unlikely.

Remember that the goal of writing is to take your readers along with you, communicate with them, and persuade them that your ideas have merit. If you insult your readers, you will not accomplish your goal. Understating your claims shows a respect for your readers' understanding and a sense of modesty on your part. Suppose, for example, that you are new to a controversy about whether a local water well should be closed because of pollution. Which of these statements would you find more credible, based on their tone and claims?

Example 3.2.4

Not understated: Anyone who says this water is safe to drink is either stupid or foolish. This toxic slop is poisoned with coliform bacteria. Don't those idiots know that?

Understated: The county says this water is drinkable, but I'm not sure I would drink it. Perhaps the county has not seen the results of the tests for harmful bacteria . . . [and so on].

Exercise 3.2.1

Rewrite each of the following sentences, changing them into understatement.
- (a) Huge amounts of money are needed to take over a media conglomerate.
- (b) I will now prove beyond any doubt that this position is correct.
- (c) A price of $23,000 for a butterfly pin is very expensive.

3.3 Litotes.

Litotes (LĪ tō tēz) is a form of understatement, created by denying the opposite of the idea in mind. Depending on the context and the subject matter, litotes either retains the effect of understatement or intensifies the expression. Compare the difference between these expressions:

Example 3.3.1

Without litotes: Those who examine themselves will gain knowledge of their failings.

With litotes: Those who examine themselves will not remain ignorant of their failings.

Example 3.3.2

Without litotes: The presence of so many security cameras in the casino meant that the man's visit was recorded.

With litotes: The presence of so many security cameras in the casino meant that the man's visit was not without record.

In the past, many writers have created litotes by using a *not un-* construction: Instead of saying, "We were willing," they would write, "We were not unwilling." In Example 3.3.2, above, the statement with litotes could have used *not unrecorded* instead of *not without record*. However, the *not un-* construction has been criticized as frequently awkward and inelegant. Often a better procedure, then, is to find an opposite word rather than to attach *un* to the word being negated. (A dictionary that includes antonyms or a synonym-antonym dictionary can be helpful here.) Instead of *not unvictorious*, you could write *not defeated*; instead of *not uninteresting*, you could write *not boring*. That said, there are occasions when the *not un-* construction is desirable because it retains some of the flavor of the original word. Consider this example from *Discourses on Art*:

Example 3.3.3

> A figure lean or corpulent, tall or short, though deviating from beauty, may still have a certain union of the various parts, which may contribute to make them on the whole not unpleasing. —Sir Joshua Reynolds

Here, *not unpleasing* seems better to convey a more exact sense of the pleasure provided by the figures than would a phrase such as *not disagreeable* or *not distasteful*.

The emphasis created by litotes can be controlled somewhat by the addition of an intensifying word or phrase that amplifies the intended meaning. Compare these effects:

Example 3.3.4

> *Litotes without intensifier:* The requirements of the contract were not disagreeable to the board.

> *Litotes with intensifier:* The requirements of the contract were not at all disagreeable to the board.

In this example, the use of the intensifying *not at all*, rather than merely *not*, amplifies the amount of agreement felt by the board. Some useful intensifiers for litotes are included in the following table.

Intensifiers for Litotes	
certainly not	not at all
definitely not	not even a little
not a bit	not in the least

Exercise 3.3.1

For each sentence below, change the underlined phrase to a negative expression of its opposite. Use an intensifier (see the table above) for at least one expression. Try to avoid the *not un-* construction.

> *Example:* The seven thousand unfilled orders represent <u>a huge backlog</u>.
> The seven thousand unfilled orders represent <u>no small backlog</u>.

(a) The problem presented by the lost files is <u>only a minor issue</u>.

(b) Unfortunately, the bread at the restaurant is <u>stale</u>.

(c) The president announced that he was <u>pessimistic</u> about next quarter's forecast.

3.4 Hyperbole.

Hyperbole (hī PUR buh lē) is exaggeration; it is the opposite of understatement. This is a challenging device to use because we live in such an overly exaggerated information environment. Between the excesses of marketing ("This is the most amazing, miracle product in the world!"), journalism ("Civilization as we know it will come to an end if this computer virus isn't stopped!"), and emotional venting ("Those morons on the court have completely shredded all our liberties once again!"), we are exposed to a constant barrage of hyperbole and have become numb toward much of it. Nevertheless, hyperbole can still be an effective tool of writing, if used carefully.

In each of the following examples, the writer is clearly exaggerating for rhetorical effect. Note that the tone is calm (not wild or angry), and each assertion is a somewhat amusing overstatement of the facts.

> **Example 3.4.1**
>
> Waiter, about this steak. I said *rare*, not *raw*. I've seen cows hurt worse than this get up and get well.

> **Example 3.4.2**
>
> There are, I suppose, a thousand excellent reasons for installing solar heating in public buildings. Using it as a means of funneling government money into a relative's bank account, however, is not one of them.

> **Example 3.4.3**
>
> At the height of the fad, every sidewalk in America was clogged with scooters rushing in every direction, to the peril of both riders and pedestrians.

When you use hyperbole, take care not to break out of your calm and moderate tone (one of the signals of reasoned discourse), and be sure that the exaggeration is of such a quality that it will not be taken literally by your readers. Rightly used in a specific place for a specific purpose, hyperbole can offer an effective touch by engaging readers' attention in a witty manner.

Exercise 3.4.1

Rewrite each of the following sentences by using hyperbole to express the underlined idea.

    (a) The Tax Simplification Act is more than <u>two thousand</u> pages long.

    (b) She's a successful agent because she knows <u>so many</u> people in the city.

    (c) <u>Not much</u> of the game was worth watching.

Style Check 3: Emphatic Positioning.

Not every part of a sentence gets the same emphasis. The most emphatic part of a sentence is at the end, while the second most emphatic part is at the beginning. Therefore, if you want to stress a word or phrase, put it at the beginning or the end of a sentence. Compare the different emphases possible by changing the order of the last words in this sentence:

Style Check Example 3.1

When she turned on the flashlight, a green frog was sitting next to her.
When she turned on the flashlight, next to her was sitting a green frog.

In the first sentence, the closeness of the frog is emphasized. In the second sentence, the frog itself is emphasized. Compare the emphases in the versions of these sentences:

Style Check Example 3.2

The counselor at last saw the happy child.
The counselor at last saw the child happy.
The counselor saw the happy child at last.
The counselor saw the child happy at last.

Use the beginning and ending of your sentences for important material, and practice moving words and phrases around to test the emphasis you want to create.

Review Questions.

1. Match each term with the description that best fits.
   _____ exaggeration for effect
   _____ an apparent meaning differing from an intended meaning
   _____ politely claiming less than what could be claimed
   _____ negating the opposite to express an idea gently
   A. litotes
   B. hyperbole
   C. understatement
   D. irony

2. Litotes
   A. always uses a *not un-* construction.
   B. understates an idea by denying its opposite.
   C. produces an ironic effect.

3. The most emphatic position in a sentence is the
   A. beginning.
   B. end.
   C. middle.

4. Match each sentence with the rhetorical device it illustrates.
   _____ No doubt everyone on the planet has now heard that song.
   _____ Jumping the canyon on a motorbike might be fun, but it would be a little risky.
   _____ "I won, I won, I'm great, I'm great," she said, not at all shyly.
   _____ At the banquet, a hundred people shared one set of salt and pepper shakers. The hotel is to be applauded for its clever cost-cutting ideas. The salt bill must be 2 percent lower this way.
   A. understatement (but not litotes)
   B. irony
   C. litotes
   D. hyperbole

Chapter 4
Transition

Reading is not a duty, and has consequently no
business to be made disagreeable.
—Augustine Birrell

One of the keys to good writing is the ability to take your reader with you as you move along in your discussion. Transitions allow you to signal clearly when you are changing direction (in subject or emphasis) and how that change connects to the previous discussion. This chapter presents several devices that help produce continuity and show logical relationship when the discussion shifts. At the end is a Style Check reminding you of the usefulness of standard logical transitions.

4.1 Metabasis.

Metabasis (muh TAB uh sis) consists of a brief statement of what has been said and what will follow. It functions as a kind of thought hinge, a transitional summary that links sections of writing together. As such, it provides great clarity by keeping the discussion ordered and focused in the reader's mind.

Example 4.1.1

We have to this point been examining the proposal advanced by Jurdane only in regard to its legal permissibility, but now we need to consider the effect it would have on research and development work in private laboratories.

Example 4.1.2

In the previous paragraphs, I have offered my analysis of the causes of this growing discontent. At this point, I would like to take up the subject of what might be done to remedy it.

Metabasis can be used to show the relationship between preceding material and an application or example.

Example 4.1.3

Now that I have made this catalog of swindles and perversions, let me give another example of the kind of writing they lead to. —George Orwell

Metabasis can also be used to sum up large sections of previous material and look forward to further extensive discussion.

Example 4.1.4
Now that we have discussed the different kinds of cactus plants available to the landscape architect, their physical requirements for sun, soil, irrigation, and drainage, and the typical design groupings selected for residential areas, we will next examine the architectural contexts that can best be enhanced by cactus planters and gardens.

Sample Phrases for Using Metabasis	
Example phrases to signal the summary	**Example phrases to signal new discussion**
Now that we have examined	It is also necessary to discuss
The discussion above has focused on	It remains for us to examine
Thus, we have now surveyed	Let us now look at
Up to this point, we have been looking at	We should now turn our attention to

There are two cautions about using metabasis. First, it should not be used frequently because of the risk of becoming mechanical. Second, since it is a summarizing device, it should have some bulk of discussion to summarize. In practice, this means that the device works much more effectively in a long paper than in a short essay. The final test is your own sense of how well the device contributes to the clarity of your presentation.

Exercise 4.1.1

For each of the following sets of ideas, incorporate the information into a transition using metabasis in a sentence or two. Feel free to use expressions from the table of sample phrases above.

(a) *Previous discussion:* The esthetics of boat design. *Next discussion:* Seaworthiness of boat design and construction.

(b) *Previous discussion:* The plan and intended results of hunger relief efforts. *Next discussion:* The logistics of delivery and distribution of food.

4.2 Procatalepsis.

Procatalepsis (prō kat uh LEP sis) anticipates an objection that might be raised by a reader and responds to it, thus permitting an argument to continue moving forward while taking into account opposing points. Skillfully used, this device can create almost a conversational effect to an argument, where opposing comments are introduced and responded to in a back-and-forth dialog.

With controversies of long standing, the objections raised may be standard ones.

Example 4.2.1

It is usually argued at this point that if the government gets out of the mail delivery business, small towns like One Tree will not have any mail service. The answer to this can be found in the history of the Pony Express. . . .

Often, a writer will invent a possible objection or difficulty in order to answer it in a way that strengthens the writer's position. In the event such an objection should arise, the reader has an answer already laid out.

Example 4.2.2

But someone might say that this battle really had no effect on the outcome of the war. Such a statement could arise only from ignoring the effect the battle had on the career of General Mars, who later became a principal figure in the decisive final conflict.

An objection can occasionally be turned into a further point of support for the writer's argument. Conceding an objection and then turning it into a point in the writer's favor can be a powerful tactic.

Example 4.2.3

A possible objection here is that this new law will make getting a driver's license much more difficult. This I freely admit and, in fact, is one of its purposes. While the new regulations may put honest people through the inconvenience of a little extra effort, the result will be nearly to eliminate the 100,000 fraudulent licenses now being issued each year.

The objection may be presented as coming from someone who misunderstands the issue at hand. The answer to the objection, then, is to clarify the actual case and remove the misunderstanding.

Example 4.2.4

Those who base their conclusions only on cost will sometimes argue that the high-speed motor is superior to the low-speed one because for the same output high-speed motors are lighter, smaller—and cheaper. However, these motors are also noisier and less efficient, and they have greater wear and shorter life. Overall, they are not superior.

When raising an objection from someone later to be revealed as mistaken or thinking poorly, be very careful not to create a straw man fallacy, where a deliberately weak argument is set up only so that the writer can knock it down. Readers can discern this technique easily, and it always reflects poorly on the writer. If your reader once begins to think, "That's not the real argument; this is a setup and a hatchet job," you have probably lost your reader's credibility. Your essay (or book) will then most likely have failed in its purpose. Similarly, do not raise an objection only to dismiss it out of hand. Always respond thoughtfully.

On the other hand, by mentioning the common and probable objections to your argument, you show that (1) you are aware of them and have considered them in the process of coming to your conclusions, and (2) there is some reasonable response to them. Answering an objection in advance weakens it should your opponent bring it up, while ignoring an objection (that someone might raise later on) could create the appearance that you are either ignorant of it or have dishonestly suppressed it. Indeed, it might be better to admit that you have only weak arguments against a common or likely objection rather than to leave it completely unmentioned.

Example 4.2.5

Those favoring the other edition argue that the same words in this text cost more money. This I admit, and it does seem unfortunate to pay twice the price for essentially the same thing. Nevertheless, this text has larger type, is bound more durably, and contains thorough and informative notes (lacking in the other). So I think it is worth the difference.

Procatalepsis usually involves raising an objection in a sentence or two. The length of the response to the objection depends on several factors: how important the objection is, what you have to say about it, and how much you think needs to be said. Sometimes a sentence or two will suffice. Often, the objection-and-answer provides the structure for a well-organized paragraph, where the objection is presented as the topic sentence and the answer fills out the paragraph. Occasionally, the objection can begin an entire section of an essay, where several following paragraphs are devoted to the response.

Exercise 4.2.1

Choose *one* of the following sets of ideas and write a few sentences developing your point a little, and then present and respond to the possible objection that someone might raise.

(a) *Your position:* Children are growing up too fast, leaving no time for childhood. *Objection:* Childhood is an outdated concept, so it does not matter if there is no time for it.

(b) *Your position:* Children are growing up at an appropriate pace. Childhood today is different from the childhood of earlier days. *Objection:* The traditional concept of a carefree childhood is important.

4.3 Hypophora.

Hypophora (hī POF or uh) involves asking one or more questions and then proceeding to answer them, usually at some length. A common usage is to ask a question at the beginning of a paragraph and then use the rest of the paragraph to answer it.

Example 4.3.1

Where else can this growing region look to augment its water supply? One possibility is the deep aquifer beneath the southeastern corner. . . .

Hypophora serves well along with the other devices in this chapter to enable a writer to clarify a chosen idea, but it has the additional benefit of helping to maintain interest. Questions quite naturally stimulate curiosity; readers who come upon a question related to the subject under discussion are therefore propelled forward by the desire to know the answer. Further, the question-and-answer structure feels natural and comfortable to most readers.

Hypophora can be used to ask a question that you believe your readers will raise during the course of reading.

Example 4.3.2

What, it might be asked, was the result of this dramatic change in tariffs on the steel industry? The annual reports for that clearly reveal. . . .

Example 4.3.3

Bacterial resistance to many antibiotics has been traced to the feeding practices in the raising of livestock, where animals are given regular doses of antibiotics in their food. But why give healthy animals a constant stream of medicine? The answer lies in the philosophy of preventive care. . . .

Hypophora can also be used to ask questions or to introduce material of importance that readers might not have the knowledge or understanding to raise themselves.

Example 4.3.4

A question of interest here would be to ask, How hot is the oven at its hottest point, when the average temperature is 425 degrees? We learned that the peak temperature occurs at. . . .

Asking a question can function as a transitional device, allowing the writer to change directions or enter a new area of discussion by asking about it.

Example 4.3.5

But here you may ask, "How can this theory be applied to the present problem?" The application comes in the form of. . . .

Questions and answers can occur in a variety of forms. As with the examples above, a single question can be raised and answered. Subsequent paragraphs might then continue with ordinary discussion, or another question might be asked and answered. In other words, part of an essay might be structured in the form of several questions and answers. A variety of this usage would be to ask all the questions at the same time and then proceed to answer them in a lengthy discussion following.

Example 4.3.6

How do we know the FTC strategy is the best, particularly in view of the complaints consumerists have made against it? Isn't there some chance that greater penalties would amount to greater deterrents? Why not get the most consumer protection simultaneously with the most punishment to offenders by easing the requirements for guilt without easing the punishment?

It happens that that's been tried, and it didn't work very well. In 1911 a law called the Printers' Ink Model Statute was proposed. . . . —Ivan L. Preston

In the example above, the writer went on for several paragraphs to discuss the case that "didn't work very well." This strategy is highly effective: The reader's curiosity is built up by a series of questions, almost guaranteeing an attentive audience for the subsequent discussion.

Hypophora can be combined with procatalepsis (see above, Section 4.2) so that an objection is raised and responded to by asking and answering a question.

Example 4.3.7

If what I say about advertising fallacies is true, why would people buy products advertised so illogically? The answer lies in human psychology. . . .

Similarly, hypophora can be combined with metabasis (see above, Section 4.1) so that the looking back is a summary and the looking forward is a question.

Example 4.3.8

To this point, we have discussed the metallurgy of the *Titanic's* rivets and the likelihood of their limited strength. Now the question arises, Did this possible weakness contribute to the ship's sinking? Our answer will come through an examination of the damage to the hull. . . .

To introduce hypophora, you can simply ask the question, as in Example 4.3.1; you can provide a question stem that formally announces that you are raising a question, as in Example 4.3.4; or you can interrupt your question with a stem, as in Example 4.3.2. You need not supply quotation marks for questions that are not attributed to others (see Examples 4.3.4 and 4.3.8). If you attribute the question to someone other than yourself, put it in quotation marks, as in Example 4.3.5. The table on the next page provides some sample question stems.

Example Question Stems for Hypophora	
A question that arises here is	Here it might be asked
At this point, you might be wondering	Here you might ask
The question might be asked at this point	Now, this raises the issue

Exercise 4.3.1

For each of the following sets of ideas, incorporate the information into a transition using hypophora. Use one sentence to ask the question and another sentence to begin an answer. Feel free to use expressions from the table of question stems above.

(a) *Question:* How music available on the Web affects CD music sales. *Answer:* Free samples can be a powerful marketing tool.

(b) *Question:* Whether there was evidence of price fixing before the current situation. *Answer:* Several claims to that effect, but never any proof.

Style Check 4: Transitions of Logic.

Transitions of logic consist of words or phrases that convey "logical intent": that is, they show the logical connection between two ideas. Since there are several possible logical connections (such as time, purpose, contrast), there are several categories of transitions of logic. The table on the next page lists many of these transitions, arranged by category and listed as milder or stronger. (Note that there is some double listing because of the different ways words can be used.) The usual advice for incorporating logical transitions into your writing follows.

1. Use transitions between paragraphs to signal connections (addition, contrast, and so forth) between idea segments. Use transitions within paragraphs to signal a change from one sentence to another or from one section of the paragraph to another.

2. Use sufficient transitions to provide coherence (holding together, like glue) and continuity (making the thought process easy to follow). Less experienced writers tend to supply too few transitions.

3. Avoid using too many strong transitions. Be careful to avoid littering your writing with *however* and *nevertheless*. Strong transitions should be used sparingly.

4. Transitions become stronger when they are placed at the beginning (or end) of a sentence, milder (or less strong) when they are moved into the sentence. Generally, moving transitions into the sentence is the better choice. See the examples below.

Style Check Example 4.1

Stronger at beginning: Another example of a succulent plant is the barrel cactus.
Milder moved inside: The barrel cactus is another example of a succulent plant.

Style Check Example 4.2

Stronger at beginning: However, American gold jewelry is less pure than European.

Less strong moved inside: American gold jewelry, however, is less pure than European.

Transitions of Logic

	Milder		Stronger	
Addition	a further x	next	additionally	first, second
	also	nor	again	further
	and	other	besides	furthermore
	and then	then	equally impor-	in addition
	another	too	tant	moreover
			finally, last	
Comparison	a similar x	just as ... so too	comparable	likewise
	another x like		in the same way	similarly
Contrast	and yet	rather	alternatively	nonetheless
	but	still	at the same time	notwithstanding
	but another	though	conversely	on the contrary
	or	yet	even so	on the other
	otherwise		for all that	hand
			however	otherwise
			in contrast	still
			instead	though this may
			nevertheless	be
Time	after	now	at last	immediately
	afterward	recently	at length	meanwhile
	before	shortly	at that time	presently
	earlier	soon	currently	subsequently
	first, second,	then	eventually	thereafter
	third	today	finally	
	later	tomorrow		
	next			
Purpose	because of this x	to do this	for that reason	to this end
			for this purpose	with this object
Place	beyond	nearby	adjacent to	in the front
	here	there	at that point	on the other side
			in the back	opposite to
Result	and so	then	accordingly	in consequence
	so		as a result	therefore
			consequently	thereupon
			hence	thus

Review Questions.

1. Study the explanations for metabasis, procatalepsis, and hypophora. All these devices share which common feature?
   A. They can be used to transition from one topic to another in an essay.
   B. They are methods of calling attention to a particular word or phrase.
   C. They all employ parallelism.

2. Match the rhetorical device with the appropriate example.

   _____ What, then, are some of the ways students can interact with each other in a distance learning program? There is a surprising number of ways. . . .

   _____ Up to this point, we have examined the associationist approach to thinking and problem solving. Let us turn now to the Gestalt school and review its contributions.

   _____ It has been objected that the hospital should not purchase a closed-tunnel MRI scanner because the scanner will not accommodate people larger than normal. The fact is, however, that surprisingly large people can still fit into the tunnel by raising their arms.
   A. metabasis
   B. procatalepsis
   C. hypophora

3. Which use of the transition of logic *also* has the mildest emphasis?
   A. Also, the sailing course includes instruction in how to tack.
   B. The sailing course also includes instruction in how to tack.
   C. The sailing course includes instruction in how to tack, also.

4. Which device can be developed either in two sentences or in an entire paragraph?
   A. metabasis
   B. procatalepsis
   C. hypophora
   D. all of the above

5. If you raised an objection and responded to it by asking a question and answering it, you would be combining which two devices?
   A. metabasis and procatalepsis
   B. metabasis and hypophora
   C. procatalepsis and hypophora

Notes

Chapter 5
Clarity

American jargon is such fun to contemplate, so full of pompous self-satisfaction on the one hand and cynical, knowing, ritual mystification on the other that description hardly knows where to begin.
—Richard Lanham, *Style: An Anti-Textbook*

Clarity—writing so that your reader has an accurate understanding of your ideas—is at the heart of good writing. The devices in this chapter will help you ensure clearer writing, allowing your reader to follow your discussion more easily, even when you need to use abstract or technical language.

5.1 Distinctio.

Distinctio (dis TINK tē ō) is the presentation of a specific meaning for a word (or reference to the various meanings of a word) in order to prevent ambiguity or confusion. Its use calls the reader's attention to the need for clarity much more deliberately than other methods of definition, such as providing synonyms during the discussion.

Ambiguous words (words with more than one possible meaning) can be clarified with distinctio.

> **Example 5.1.1**
> *Ambiguous:* It is impossible to make methanol for twenty-five cents a gallon.
> *Clarified with distinctio:* To make methanol for twenty-five cents a gallon is impossible; by *impossible* I mean currently beyond our technological capabilities.

In the example above, note that the word *impossible* can mean either *cannot be done now* or *cannot be done ever*. The use of distinctio clarifies which meaning is intended.

Distinctio is especially useful for clarifying the use of words that are by their nature vague or imprecise, such as *quickly* and *modern automobile* in the examples below. The clarification assures that your readers know what you mean when you use the word.

> **Example 5.1.2**
> *Ambiguous:* Move the precipitate from the filter paper to the crucible quickly.
> *Clarified with distinctio:* Move the precipitate from the filter paper to the crucible quickly—that is, within three minutes.

Example 5.1.3

Ambiguous: The modern automobile requires substantial technical expertise to repair.

Clarified with distinctio: The modern automobile (and here I refer to post-1985 vehicles with computer-controlled engines and transmissions) requires substantial technical expertise to repair.

Distinctio can involve the discussion of more than one meaning of a word, in a sorting-out process of analyzing the statements of another writer. You can suggest that the other writer is being ambiguous and that, in order for you to respond to the statement, some clarification must first be made.

Example 5.1.4

Several board members have described the process as a simple one. If by simple they mean easy to explain on paper, they are correct. But if they mean there are no complexities involved in getting the system to work, they are quite mistaken.

A final use for distinctio is to supply the definition for a technical term or other word that some of your readers may not know. A simple clarification can prevent readers from stumbling over an unfamiliar term.

Example 5.1.5

Popular in the Renaissance was a euphuistic style—that is, a highly ornate and excessively rhetorical prose modeled after John Lyly's book, *Euphues.*

Many words are general or abstract, making them subject to varied interpretation. Adding clarification to prevent misunderstanding of important terms can be a substantial help to your reader. Note that in many cases the definition or explanation takes place in the same sentence as the presentation of the term. You usually do not need to interrupt your discourse with a separate sentence of definition.

Below is a table listing some of the phrases useful for introducing distinctio. You will no doubt find others and create variations on those here. As always, practice these and find the ones that best suit your own writing voice.

Sample Phrases for Introducing Distinctio	
by X I mean	that is
for our purposes, X refers to	the meaning for X being
here we will define X to mean	which is to say
in this case, X refers to	X here must be taken to mean
in this context, X means	X here should not be taken to mean

Exercise 5.1.1

Rewrite each of these sentences, adding distinctio to specify a particular meaning of the underlined word or phrase.

(a) When you take the truck down the mountain, do not drive <u>too fast</u>.

(b) I'd like to buy an <u>inexpensive</u> car.

(c) The furniture in that store seems rather <u>old-fashioned</u>.

5.2 Exemplum.

While distinctio (above) offers a clarifying definition of a term, exemplum (eg ZEM plum) provides a specific example. Examples often include the visual, concrete, specific details that a reader can see in the mind's eye. Our minds process ideas more easily if those ideas are connected to pictures. Purely abstract discussions are often difficult to follow, but they can be made easier by the presence of a pertinent case, an application, story, or other kind of example.

So useful for clarification is exemplum that this book is built on its use: Every device here is illustrated by examples. Note below how examples can clarify a discussion.

Example 5.2.1

A powerful way to gain the attention of adults is to involve their children. Warnings to protect children are more interesting and important than warnings to adults alone. For example, a label on a hair dryer in a hotel reads, "Warn children of the risk of death by electrical shock." This language gets the close attention not only of parents but also of adults without children.

Example 5.2.2

Snow cone flavors, such as *bubblegum* and *mango*, are often named after candy or fruit.

Example 5.2.3

The conifers (evergreens like pine and cypress trees) produce seeds in hard, cone-shaped structures.

Usually, examples are built into a paragraph rather than set off (as in this book) because, as the examples above show, an example is often quite brief. Many times, only a phrase or a sentence or two is needed. A longer example can be presented in its own paragraph.

On the next page is a table of a few useful ways to introduce exemplum.

Sample Phrases for Introducing Exemplum	
a case in point	for instance
a hypothetical case might be	such as
a typical situation might be	this might be shown by
as can be seen in	to illustrate
for example	X would be an example

Note: The abbreviation *e.g.* (for the Latin, *exempli gratia*) instead of *for example* is now often viewed as somewhat stilted, as is the use of *i.e.* (*id est*) for *that is*. As prose styles have modernized and simplified, many Latin abbreviations have fallen into disuse. We no longer encounter *viz.* (*videlicet*, meaning *namely*) in contemporary writing, while *q.v.* (*quod vide*, meaning *which see*) lives on only in highly formal writing. Similarly, most writers now use *above* and *below* rather than *supra* and *infra*. Even the use of *etc.* (*et cetera*, meaning *and others*) often gives way to *and so forth* or even *and others*. All this is to say that the use of *e.g.* is not recommended. There are more effective choices.

Exercise 5.2.1

For each of the following sentences, add an example suggested by the idea in parentheses. You may revise the sentence and include the example or write a second sentence containing the example.

(a) This side of the house needs some greenery. (two specific plants or trees)

(b) I remember that town by its odors. (one particular smell on Main Street)

(c) There are many alternatives to carbonated beverages. (three other kinds of non-alcoholic beverages)

5.3. Amplification.

Amplification consists of restating a word or idea and adding more detail. This device allows a writer to call attention to an expression that may otherwise be passed over, and is therefore useful for both clarity and emphasis. The effect is also one of slowing down the process of thought, as the writer seems to back up a bit, restate a term, and provide detail about it before continuing the discussion.

Example 5.3.1

In my hunger after ten days of overly rigorous dieting, I saw visions of ice cream—mountains of creamy, luscious ice cream, dripping with gooey syrup and calories.

Example 5.3.2

The speaker illustrated his presentation with slides—color slides, text slides, drawings, photographs, slides with video clips, musical slides, altogether too many slides—and spoke as if we already knew the material.

Example 5.3.3

The subway car came to a halt with a jolt: a wrenching, neck-snapping jolt.

Note that by holding back some of the detail until after the first presentation of the idea, the writer can create a more vivid effect: First the idea in general is presented, and then a clearer or more specific version.

Example 5.3.4

The abandoned pipe had been overcome by rust—red-brown, bumpy, flaky, steel-eating rust—that slowly consumed the very essence of the pipe.

The usual caution is not to overdo amplification. With some creativity, a writer could continue to amplify an idea into several paragraphs, but the result would be to add obfuscation rather than clarity to it. In fact, amplification on steroids helped produce the style known as euphuism (see Example 5.1.5 earlier), which became popular in Elizabethan England, but which also helped give rhetoric a bad name. Do use amplification—along with good judgment.

Exercise 5.3.1

Rewrite each of the following sentences, adding amplification to the underlined term.
- (a) Consumers have been interested in this <u>perfume</u> in record numbers.
- (b) Last year the winter was unusually <u>cold.</u>
- (c) From the landing, she looked up at the <u>stairs</u> and wondered how long the climb would take.

5.4 Metanoia.

Metanoia (met uh NOI uh) qualifies a statement or part of a statement by rejecting it or calling it back and expressing it in a better, milder, or stronger way.

Example 5.4.1

The most important quality to look for in impact sockets is hardness; no, not so much hardness as resistance to shock and shattering.

Example 5.4.2

Most bottled water companies try to capture the mountain spring water taste; or rather, they do not so much capture it as manufacture it by adding minerals and ozone.

The effect of metanoia is to provide emphasis (by fussing over a term and redefining it), clarity (by providing the improved definition), and a sense of spontaneity (the reader is thinking along with the writer as the writer revises a passage). This correction of a statement is an imitation of speech, of course, where extemporaneous speakers often adjust their thoughts and sentences as they proceed. Thus, a device that is actually quite deliberate and calculated can give the impression of naturalness.

Metanoia can move from restrained to more aggressive.

Example 5.4.3

These new textbooks will genuinely improve the lives of our children, or rather the children of the whole district.

Example 5.4.4

If we did not foresee the loss of this account, it is our own fault for failing to see the hints—no, the flashing neon signs—that warned us what was coming.

Or it can be used to tone down and qualify an overly ambitious statement (while at the same time retaining the force of the original expression).

Example 5.4.5

While the crack widens and the cliff every minute comes closer to crashing down around us, the officials are just standing around twiddling their thumbs, or at least they have been singularly unresponsive to our appeals for action.

In the past, the most common word used for invoking metanoia was *nay*, but this word has become archaic and is thus not commonly used by modern writers. Instead, there are several other useful words and phrases for indicating the recall and restatement, as shown in the table below.

Words and Phrases for Metanoia	
I mean	or if not X then Y
I should say	or maybe
no	or more accurately
not so much X as Y	or perhaps
or at least	or rather
or better	to be more exact

Exercise 5.4.1

For each sentence below, add metanoia that calls back the underlined word and offers another word based on the idea in parentheses.

Example:

This new dessert tastes <u>terrible.</u> (less than terrible)

This new dessert tastes terrible—or perhaps I should say interesting in a disagreeable way.

(a) The team ended the quarter with a very <u>skillful</u> shot. (it was not skill at all)

(b) At that price we would <u>lose</u> money. (not actually losing)

(c) The new play equipment will make <u>kids</u> happy. (more people than just kids)

Exercise 5.4.2

Write three sentences incorporating metanoia according to the descriptions below.

(a) Call back a more dramatic or exaggerated term and substitute a more reserved one.

(b) Call back a more reserved term and express the idea in a more dramatic way.

(c) Qualify an entire idea rather than just a word (as in Example 5.4.5).

Style Check 5: Clear versus Opaque Writing.

Every discipline has its own useful jargon, and difficult concepts often require abstract language. However, neither jargon nor abstract language should be used as ends in themselves or for the purpose of "ritual mystification" (see the epigraph at the beginning of this chapter). While some writers use language for posturing—to show off—or to make their ideas appear as sophisticated as possible, the best writing strives to make complex ideas less difficult to comprehend, not more difficult. A large vocabulary is valuable because it allows more precise thinking and writing. Having the exact word for an idea will strengthen your writing remarkably. The caution is that you should use words for the benefit of their precision, and not for their rarity or number of syllables.

Clarity is partly a function of audience, and that is why every writing teacher tells students to consider their audience before writing. What is clear to an audience of professionals in the discipline may not be clear to a general audience. You will need to adjust your level of explanation, definition, examples, and vocabulary to match the audience you are addressing. Whoever your audience is, though, your primary question should always be, "Am I communicating clearly?" Try focusing on your reader rather than yourself. Instead of asking, "Am I saying what I want?" ask yourself, "Will my reader understand what I am saying?"

Review Questions.

1. Study the explanations for distinctio, amplification, and metanoia. All these devices share which common feature?
   A. They create transitions between sections of an essay.
   B. Their principal function is decoration (making the writing more attractive).
   C. They help define or clarify a word or idea.

2. Which device would be most useful for creating the impression of thinking out loud—that is, of revising your ideas as you write?
   A. distinctio
   B. exemplum
   C. metanoia

3. Match the device to its introductory cue.
   _____ take, for example, the case of
   _____ or perhaps I should say
   _____ by which I mean
   A. distinctio
   B. exemplum
   C. metanoia

4. Amplification is useful for clarifying an idea and also for
   A. emphasizing an idea that might otherwise be passed by without much attention.
   B. recalling an idea that was too extreme and replacing it with one that is more modest.
   C. filling out the answer to a question at some length.

5. Clarity in writing is influenced by
   A. choice of words (language).
   B. audience (the reader or hearer).
   C. both A and B.

Chapter 6
Figurative Language I

It's important to learn to use all the devices I have
discussed, . . . but the most important thing by far
is to master the use of metaphor.
—Aristotle, *Poetics*

Clarifying the unfamiliar by comparing it with the familiar is one of the key methods
of teaching and learning. The devices presented in this and the following two chapters
all embody this method, for they are all devices of association. An idea under discussion
is illuminated or made more vivid through an imaginative comparison with something
already familiar to the reader. These devices are among the most creative tools available
to a writer.

6.1 Simile.

A simile (SIM uh lē) compares two very different things that have at least one quality
in common. While similes are used in poetry principally for artistic effect, in formal writing they serve not only to increase interest but also to clarify an idea in an imaginative
way.

> **Example 6.1.1**
> After long exposure to the direct sun, the leaves of the houseplant looked
> like pieces of overcooked bacon.

In the simile above, the subject to be compared is *the leaves of the houseplant*, while the
image used is *pieces of overcooked bacon*. The word that directly expresses the comparison
is *like*. In this instance, the writer wanted to emphasize the shriveled and brown look of
the leaves, so a familiar, vivid image was chosen. Most people know what overcooked
bacon looks like, so the image effectively presents a visual idea to the mind's eye.

Similes are imaginative comparisons between two fundamentally different things,
not between genuinely similar ones. In fact, if the things compared are too much like
each other, the comparison is not a simile. For example, the comparison, "The office
building on Main Street is like the warehouse on Perimeter Road," is not a simile because a building and a warehouse are too much alike.

The two guidelines for creating a simile, then, are these:

◆ **The image must be familiar.** Because the goal of the simile is to illuminate the
subject, the image must be more familiar than the subject. Vivid, striking images

47

that your readers know well—without being cliché—are the best. Look for the visual appeal.

♦ **The difference between subject and image should be substantial.** It is tempting to say that the greater the difference between the two, the more artistic, effective, and brilliant the simile will be. However, the point or points of similarity must still connect the subject and image in a workable way.

Because the comparison in a simile is most often directly expressed (that is, the comparison is formally introduced), an invoking or introducing word is usually present. When a noun is compared to a noun, the simile is normally introduced by *like*.

Example 6.1.2
In Mrs. Johnson's class, the students sat upright in straight and even rows, like books on a shelf.

Example 6.1.3
Like the web of a drunken spider, the new organizational chart seemed to lack careful planning.

When a verb or clause is compared to another verb or clause, the simile is most often introduced by *as*.

Example 6.1.4
Even after the avalanche, the climbers remained constantly attentive to their goal, as a sunflower continues to stay focused on the sun.

Example 6.1.5
Just as a pencil sharpener grinds away the excess wood and pencil lead to form a new, sharp point, so the copy editor trimmed the surplus text to create a pointed, direct story.

When an adjective or adverb forms the subject of the comparison, the simile is usually formed with an *as . . . as* construction.

Example 6.1.6
His greeting was as sudden as an unexpected honk.

As Examples 6.1.3 and 6.1.5 above show, the image of the simile can precede the subject. When the image comes first and the simile uses a verb clause (as in Example 6.1.5), the simile is shown by an *as . . . so* construction. In practice, either the *as* or the *so* is often omitted, in order to avoid an old-fashioned, proverblike feeling.

Example 6.1.7

As and *so* present: As a battery-powered toy starts out strong and then fades, so did the assessment project.

As omitted: A battery-powered toy starts out strong and then fades; so did the assessment project.

So omitted: As a battery-powered toy starts out strong and then fades, the assessment project did, too.

Many times, the subject and the image of a simile are so different that the point of similarity is not clear unless it is provided. In such cases, the similarity can be stated in a way that applies to both subject and image.

Example 6.1.8

Money is like fertilizer—it's not any good unless you spread it around.
—Adapted from Francis Bacon

Example 6.1.9

Like a skunk, he suffered from bad publicity for one noticeable flaw, but bore no one any ill will.

Example 6.1.10

We cannot treat our most experienced engineers like old tools that have given years of faithful service only to be put on a shelf and forgotten merely because we have new ones.

Sometimes the point or points of similarity will be presented only in terms of the image itself, requiring the reader to translate it in terms of the subject.

Example 6.1.11

People are like stereo speakers: A fancy grille does not guarantee a good sound.

In the example above, the reader must translate the meaning of *fancy grille* to the application of people (namely, their external appearance) as well as the meaning of *good sound* (goodness or kindness).

The point of similarity is sometimes expressed in just a word or two. Compare the difference between each pair of similes in the examples below, and note how just a word or two can make the comparison much clearer.

Example 6.1.12

The pitching mound is like a camel's back.
The pitching mound is humped too much like a camel's back.

Example 6.1.13

I see men, but they look like trees.

I see men, but they look like trees, walking. —Mark 8:24 (RSV)

Note that in the example above, the qualifying word *walking* not only clarifies the point of similarity but also draws the subject and image closer together by making the image more similar to the subject (the men are not like just any trees, but like *walking* trees).

The image can even be compressed into an adjective describing the subject word.

Example 6.1.14

The argument of this book uses a pretzel-like logic.

Example 6.1.15

The reducing gear in the transmission has a flowerlike symmetry.

Similes can be negative, asserting that the subject and image are unlike each other in one or more ways.

Example 6.1.16

The new version is good, but the software is no longer as speedy as a bullet.

Example 6.1.17

The stock collapsed because the chief executive of the company failed to realize that accounting is nothing like preparing food: Cooking dinner makes a meal, but cooking the books makes a felon.

In addition to using *like* or *as*, there are several other ways to create a simile.

Example 6.1.18

Her voice was more gentle than the fall of a rose petal on the softest moss.

Example 6.1.19

His temper reminds me of a volcano; his heart, of a rock; his personality, of sandpaper.

Example 6.1.18 above also serves to point out that the image in a simile does not always provide a specific clarification of the subject. Often, the image is suggestive, even ambiguous. In this example, no one can say exactly how gentle the fall of a rose petal on soft moss really is, but every reader gets the general idea, elegantly expressed, of a high degree of gentleness. If the writer had written *very gentle* instead, a similar inexactness would result (for just how gentle is *very gentle*?), yet without any elegance.

The table on the next page lists some of the possible ways of comparing the subject to the image in a simile.

Some Methods for Constructing Similes		
X is like Y	X is not like Y	X is the same as Y
X is more than Y	X is less than Y	X does Z; so does Y
X is similar to Y	X resembles Y	X is as Z as Y
X is Z like Y	X is more Z than Y	X is less Z than Y
as Y, so X	X, as if Y	X makes me think of Y

Occasionally, a simile can be created without any comparative word. Similes like this are said to be submerged.

Example 6.1.20
Baby Anna has silky hair and the skin of an angel.

In the example above, the similes are *hair like silk* and *skin like an angel's skin*. In neither case is the comparing word *like* necessary, thus allowing a greater economy of expression.

When you create your own similes, pay attention not just to the point of similarity you wish to convey but to the qualities suggested by the image as a whole. Those qualities transfer over to the subject and influence how the subject is understood. Compare the widely different effects created by the similes in the example below.

Example 6.1.21
That student group is spreading like wildfire.
That student group is spreading like cancer.
That student group is really blossoming now.
That student group, like an amoeba, is engulfing the campus.

Therefore, when you create a simile, consider the effect you want to produce—a visual scene, an emotional touch, a positive or negative feeling—and select an image that will be appropriate to your need.

Exercise 6.1.1

Rewrite the following sentences, incorporating a simile suggested by the idea in parentheses.

(a) The service in this restaurant is slow. (a slow-flowing liquid in a winter month)
(b) Before he could get to work, his ideas dissipated. (a liquid on something porous)

6.2 Analogy.

An analogy (uh NAL uh jē), like a simile, compares two different things by identifying points of similarity. The differences between a simile and an analogy are several:

♦ An analogy usually identifies several points of similarity, rather than just one or two identified in a simile.

♦ An analogy is created for the purpose of giving conceptual clarity, explaining an unfamiliar idea by comparing it to a familiar one.

♦ An analogy is a practical device used to help the reader's thought process, and is therefore usually chosen for its close similarity to the subject, so that the qualities in common offer helpful illumination of the subject. Similes more often strive for effect through the use of images very different from the subjects.

Analogies are useful for explaining technical information or processes in a way that a general reader can understand.

Example 6.2.1

Flash memory chips work like a chalkboard, in that, when information is written on it, the information remains present even when the power is turned off. Only when the information is deliberately erased will it disappear. And like the chalkboard, flash memory can be written on and erased many times.

Example 6.2.2

The oil system of an automobile is similar to the circulatory system of the body. The oil system has tubes and passages for the oil in the same way the body has blood vessels. The engine drives an oil pump to circulate the oil, corresponding to the action of the heart. And, just as the kidneys clean the blood as it passes through, the oil filter cleans the circulating oil.

Analogies are also useful for connecting abstract concepts to concrete pictures. Apprehending a concept is easier for most people if they can attach a picture to an idea. Analogies serve this purpose.

Example 6.2.3

A virtual device, like an impersonator, pretends to be something other than it really is. For example, just as a cab driver with the aid of a lab coat may impersonate a doctor, an area of computer memory with the aid of software can impersonate a disk drive. The computer uses this pretended drive as if the drive were a real piece of hardware, but it is only virtual hardware.

Example 6.2.4

In order to solve a problem, you first have to know what the problem really is, in the same way that you can't untie a knot until you've found the knot.
—Aristotle

In the example above, Aristotle attaches his abstract comment about problem solving to the familiar image of untying a knot. The analogy thereby clarifies his point about the need to identify problems before attempting to act on them.

Some analogies draw an extended parallel between the abstract idea and the concrete images that clarify it. Note the several points of similarity between ideas in this passage from *A Tale of a Tub*:

Example 6.2.5

I conceive therefore, as to the business of being profound, that it is with writers, as with wells; a person with good eyes may see to the bottom of the deepest, provided any water be there; and, that often, when there is nothing in the world at the bottom, besides dryness and dirt, tho' it be but a yard and [a] half under ground, it shall pass, however, for wondrous deep, upon no wiser a reason than because it is wondrous dark. —Jonathan Swift

Especially in argumentative writing, analogies should be used carefully, serving as aids to thinking rather than as substitutes for argument. The logical fallacy of *faulty analogy* occurs when an analogy is brought in to substitute for genuine argument.

Example 6.2.6

Faulty analogy: We should get rid of those old, worn-out books in the library. After all, you don't keep worn-out socks in your dresser drawer. You get rid of them.

This analogy is faulty because it substitutes an image for a reason or argument and because the differences between the subject and image are so substantial that the argument does not hold. (We continue to use old books, which retain value, while we do not continue to use old socks.) The appeal of a faulty analogy is that the image can be constructed in a way that it is obviously true. We do, indeed, get rid of worn-out socks. However, the image of an analogy should not be used as if it were evidence.

Analogies are valuable in writing when they are used to explain a thought process or clarify a line of reasoning. They are among the most pleasant teaching tools, helping readers come to understanding through an almost storylike process. Seventeenth-century poet George Herbert tells us that "people by what they understand are best led to what they understand not," and eighteenth-century writer Samuel Johnson adds that analogies have "always been the most popular and efficacious art of instruction." Used appropriately, they can bring understanding and context to difficult ideas. Their visual qualities put genuine meaning into the expression, "Now I see!"

Exercise 6.2.1

Revise the following sentences, adding analogies by incorporating an image and points of similarity suggested by the idea in parentheses. Use more than one sentence, if you want.

(a) The nutrition book guides you through the steps toward a healthy body. (something that guides you or tells you how to get somewhere or follow instructions)

(b) An electrician installs a circuit breaker on house wiring to protect the wiring, not people, when there is a short. The electrician installs a ground-fault interrupter to protect people. (A car's bumper protects the car, not the driver, in an accident. The airbag protects the driver.)

6.3 Metaphor.

A metaphor (MET uh for), like its relatives simile and analogy described in the sections above, compares two different things. The significant difference, though, is that a metaphor *identifies* the subject with the image: That is, instead of saying that the subject is *like* the image, a metaphor asserts that the subject is the image in some sense.

Example 6.3.1

Simile: A good book is like a friend.
Metaphor: A good book is a friend.

Example 6.3.2

The mind is but a barren soil; a soil which is soon exhausted and will produce no crop, or only one, unless it be continually fertilized and enriched with foreign matter. —Joshua Reynolds

In this example, Reynolds asserts that the mind *is* a barren soil, not that it is *like* a barren soil. Of course, he means that the two are alike in some way, but the equation of the two with a metaphor produces a more dramatic effect than would the use of a simile. More of the qualities of the image are transferred to the subject through a metaphor than usually are through a simile. Notice the power of metaphorical identification in this example from *Pensees*:

Example 6.3.3

What sort of a monster then is man? What a novelty, what a portent, what a chaos, what a mass of contradictions, what a prodigy! Judge of all things, a ridiculous earthworm who is the repository of truth, a sink of uncertainty and error; the glory and the scum of the world. —Blaise Pascal, tr. Martin Turnell

A common construction for metaphor is the use of the *to be* verb, to equate the subject and the image by saying that the subject *is* the image.

Example 6.3.4

If we are going to make ecological progress on an international scale, we must get over the belief that the ocean is the world's trash can.

Example 6.3.5

I like listening to this music: It's my morning cup of coffee.

Metaphors, like similes and analogies, can also be negative. The subject is clarified by naming but rejecting an image. Sometimes another image is substituted, in a manner suggestive of a metanoia (see Chapter 5, Section 5.4).

Example 6.3.6

A college degree by itself will not buy a ticket to the Island of Easy Living.

Example 6.3.7

Her comments were not a river of criticism intended to quench their burning plan. Rather, they were a much-needed splash of cold water in the face, waking the team up to the reality of the challenge.

Another method of constructing metaphors is to create a possessive construction, where the image is declared to be part of the subject or owned by the subject. Typical phrasings are *the [image] of [subject]* and *the [subject]'s [image]*, as in the following examples, where the metaphors are underlined.

Example 6.3.8

The <u>fountain of knowledge</u> will dry up unless it is continuously replenished by streams of new learning.

Example 6.3.9

The first <u>beam of hope</u> that had ever darted into his mind rekindled youth in his cheeks and doubled the lustre of his eyes. —Samuel Johnson

Example 6.3.10

<u>The police department's golden key to the heart of the neighborhood</u> was the establishment of walking beats and getting to know the citizens.

A metaphor can be constructed for a subject by choosing a verb that belongs to the image, thereby talking about the subject in terms of the image. In the following example, the subject *words* is being metaphorically compared to a person or animal that can limp.

Example 6.3.11

On the stand, the witness's words limped out with a lack of conviction.

The many ways of constructing a metaphor allow for great flexibility. Compare the degrees of directness in the identification of subject and image in the following examples. First, here is a fully direct identification (pirates are leeches):

Example 6.3.12

At the annual meeting, the executive said, "Software pirates are the leeches of our bottom line, sucking the blood out of our company."

Here is semi-implied (an unstated person is a motormouth):

Example 6.3.13

Around the conference table, more than one delegate wondered when the motormouth would run out of fuel.

Here is implied (*wing* and *fly* imply birds; the persons are birds):

Example 6.3.14

Thank you for taking Ted under your wing. He has adapted to the new culture quickly as a result. Soon he will be ready to fly.

Here is highly implied (music implicitly equated with good economic times):

Example 6.3.15

If consumers are holding back on purchases when the music is still playing, how will they behave when the music stops?

In this last example, the metaphor contains only the image and not the subject: Music playing refers to good economic times and music stopping refers to difficult economic times, but the equation is not expressed directly. If you construct highly implied metaphors like this, take steps to ensure that the context makes the metaphor understandable.

A final aspect of implied metaphors is that the image itself may be imprecise.

Example 6.3.16

When she saw the last winning number in that night's lottery drawing, her face wilted.

Example 6.3.17

The scientist became enraged when anyone suggested that there was even the slightest crack in his theory.

In Example 6.3.16 above, the metaphor compares the woman's face to a plant that can wilt. What kind of plant is left unstated. In Example 6.3.17, the metaphor compares the scientist's theory to something that can crack, where a crack indicates a flaw or weakness. Whether that object is a concrete wall, a vase, a window pane, or some other item is not stated. The ambiguity allows the important attribute (such as crackability) to transfer, while keeping other attributes hidden. As a result, the image is quick and direct, with little or none of the complexity that might be added by a more complete image.

The following table presents some example ways of connecting subject and image in a metaphor, using the subject of *life* and the image of a *river*.

Example Methods for Constructing Metaphors		
life is a river	the river of life	life's river
life flows	swimming upstream in life	a flowing life

When you construct metaphors, remember that the qualities of the image transfer to the subject even more powerfully than with the use of a simile (because the metaphor equates the subject and the image in an imaginative sense). Take care, then, that the connotative feel of the transfer (positive, negative, emotional, sensual, comical, and so on) accords with your intentions for the effect. Strive for freshness and originality in your imagery. Our language includes many worn-out metaphors that have become tiresomely cliché and should be ignored in favor of more original ones.

Exercise 6.3.1

For each item below, use the subject and image to create a metaphor. Write a complete sentence in each case.

(a) *Subject:* the food at the hotel. *Image:* a magnet.

(b) *Subject:* the amount of new work being assigned. *Image:* an overloaded dump truck.

Exercise 6.3.2

Choose a metaphor of your own and write a sentence expressing the metaphor in each form described below.

(a) the image of subject (for example, "the anchor of hope")

(b) the subject's image (for example, "hope's anchor")

(c) the subject is the image (for example, "hope is an anchor")

6.4 Catachresis.

Catachresis (kat uh KRĒ sis) is a striking, even extreme, implied metaphor that often makes use of a grammatical misconstruction. The combination of a metaphor and the unusual expression can be dramatically effective. One way to construct a catachresis is to substitute an associated thing for the intended idea.

> **Example 6.4.1**
>
> I will speak daggers to her, but use none. —*Hamlet*, 3.2.414

In the example above, Hamlet substitutes *daggers* for the idea of *angry words* or even threatening death with daggers.

> **Example 6.4.2**
>
> Blind mouths! That scarce themselves know how to hold
> A sheep-hook, or have learned aught else the least
> That to the faithful herdman's art belongs! —John Milton

In the example above, Milton substitutes *blind* for the idea of ignorant speech coming from the mouths of false teachers.

Another common method of producing a catachretic metaphor is to use one part of speech metaphorically for another (see anthimeria, Chapter 16, Section 16.3). In the following examples, nouns (*words* and *turtled*) are used as verbs.

> **Example 6.4.3**
>
> He words me, girls, he words me. —*Antony and Cleopatra*, 5.2.191

> **Example 6.4.4**
>
> The little old lady turtled along at ten miles per hour.

Catachresis can also be used to describe a mixed metaphor, where two or more metaphors interact, resulting in a bizarre and often comical effect.

> **Example 6.4.5**
>
> The fascist octopus has sung its swan song. —George Orwell

> **Example 6.4.6**
>
> The strong arm of the law will not dance to that tune.

In Example 6.4.5 above, Orwell quotes this particular mixed metaphor (in his essay, "Politics and the English Language") to point out that metaphor mixers often are not even thinking about what they write. The statement that an octopus has sung (and sung like a swan, no less) creates a grotesque image for the reader. The same grotesqueness is produced in Example 6.4.6 by the image of an arm dancing.

Mixed metaphors are often the result of the image of one metaphor becoming the subject of another metaphor: Fascism is an octopus and the octopus is singing, or the law is a strong arm and the arm is dancing. Usually, mixing metaphors is a sign of thoughtless haste rather than rhetorical prowess, so be careful if you construct them with intent. Deliberate mixed metaphors should be obviously bizarre and comical, in order to give away the author's intent. Adding a "so to speak" or "as someone said" (and then quoting the mixed metaphor) will reveal to your readers that you are mixing intentionally and for effect.

Exercise 6.4.1

Revise each of these sentences by substituting another example of catachresis for the underlined word, according to the instructions in parentheses.

Example model: I will speak <u>daggers</u> to her, but use none. (a pleasant noun)

Example revision: I will speak flowers to her, but give none.

(a) He <u>words</u> me, girls. He <u>words</u> me. (a noun implying *shuts me out*)
(b) The little old lady <u>turtled</u> along at ten miles per hour. (another slow animal)

Style Check 6: Demetrius on Metaphor.

Demetrius offers two useful ideas for constructing metaphors. First, he says that when there is a great difference between the size (or importance) of the subject and the image, the image chosen should be greater or more sweeping than the subject. In other words, the subject should be smaller than the image so that an important subject will not be trivialized by a small image illuminating it. In each of the following two examples, Demetrius would recommend the first expression but not the second.

Style Check Example 6.1

Subject (tears) smaller than image (waterfall): The tears cascaded down her cheek.

Subject (waterfall) larger than image (tears): The waterfall wept down the rock.

Style Check Example 6.2

Subject (editing) smaller than image (surgery): Editing down the document required extensive surgery.

Subject (amputating) larger than image (editing): Amputating the leg was a lengthy edit.

When the desired effect is to reduce the importance of the subject, however, using a subject with a lesser image can be effective.

Style Check Example 6.3

Subject (cleaning house) less than image (tornado): Stand back: She's a tornado when she cleans house.

Subject (tornado) greater than image (cleaning house): That tornado last week really did a housecleaning job on the west end of town.

Style Check Example 6.4

Subject (executive career) less than image (meteor): The executive had a meteoric career.

Subject (meteor) greater than image (career): The meteor had a short career.

The second point Demetrius makes is that overly strong metaphors can be softened by adding an adjective that brings the image and subject closer together.

Style Check Example 6.5

Without adjective: The muddy tires made the car appear to be sitting on pizzas.

With adjective: The muddy tires made the car appear to be sitting on rubber pizzas.

Style Check Example 6.6

Without adjective: Her words were an ointment that calmed him.

With adjective: Her words were a verbal ointment that calmed him.

Review Questions.

1. For each example, place an *S* in the blank if a simile is used, an *M* if a metaphor is used, and *N* if neither simile nor metaphor is present.

_____ This video series will be a magic carpet that takes viewers to distant lands.

_____ My hair looks like the thorns on a barrel cactus today.

_____ Just as the rocks at the beach withstand the crashing of the waves, the committee stood up to the criticism of its report.

_____ The candle burned all night until the wax was completely gone.

_____ The voice of time is so soft that we seldom hear its call.

2. An analogy differs from a simile in that an analogy
   A. has fewer points of similarity between subject and image.
   B. is more artistic than a simile.
   C. is constructed principally to provide conceptual clarity to an idea.

3. A faulty analogy is

   A. a logical fallacy.

   B. an analogy that does not make sense.

   C. an analogy that criticizes the faults in something.

4. Match the rhetorical device with the appropriate example.

   _____ The boss dropped the news like a bomb.

   _____ Their ears listened to our plea for help, but their hands were deaf.

   _____ Technology's children are now everywhere among us.

   _____ A falsehood could be an honest mistake, just as a misprint is an unintended error.

   A. simile

   B. analogy

   C. metaphor

   D. catachresis

5. For each example below, write *MM* if the sentence contains a mixed metaphor. Write *OK* if the metaphor in the sentence is not mixed.

   _____ She never leaves the highway of her main point to detour into a dusty old digressive road.

   _____ Hitting the witness with the club of this letter ought to wash his face of those lies.

   _____ Thanks for shining a light on this project and illuminating the direction we need to take.

   _____ Management has drawn up an airtight plan that we can use to strain out the flaws in the production process.

6. How does Demetrius say that a metaphor can be made softer or less dramatic?

   A. by choosing everyday images that will be familiar to every reader

   B. by using very few metaphors in a given essay

   C. by adding an adjective that brings subject and image closer together

Notes

Chapter 7
Figurative Language II

Metaphor, more than anything else, contributes to
a clear and distinctive and appealing style.
—Aristotle, *Rhetoric*

A skillful use of imagery does much more than provide clarity and vividness to writing. Used well, these devices can add richness, texture, and interest to prose that might otherwise be bald, sterile, even boring. Beautiful and thought provoking, the devices in this chapter are all subtypes of metaphor, providing additional powerful tools for effective writing.

7.1 Metonymy.

Metonymy (muh TAHN uh mē) is a type of metaphor in which something closely associated with another thing is named instead of the other thing. In other words, an associated idea is substituted for the subject idea.

Example 7.1.1
The pen is mightier than the sword. —Edward Bulwer-Lytton

In the example above, a pen is closely associated with writing—or better, ideas—and a sword is closely associated with warfare. Thus, Bulwer-Lytton is telling us that ideas are more powerful than warfare.

Example 7.1.2
This land belongs to the crown. [*crown* substituted for *king*]

Example 7.1.3
Flight simulators are valuable because you can die in software and still be around to fly another day. [*software* substituted for *a simulated air crash*]

Example 7.1.4
By the sweat of your face you will eat bread. —Genesis 3:19 (NASB) [*sweat of your face* substituted for *hard labor*]

As Example 7.1.4 above shows, the substituted idea in a metonymy is often more vivid and concrete than the subject idea. *Sweat of your face* is highly pictorial and, in fact, something most people have experienced. *Hard labor*, on the other hand, is an abstraction that does not produce such a specific, gripping image.

Another benefit of metonymy is that the image can provide a specific focus for a more general subject idea.

> **Example 7.1.5**
> You cannot fight city hall.

In this example, *city hall* is a substitution not merely for one agency or one official but for the processes of government (a vague abstraction). Rather than attempt to conceptualize the operations of government, the reader can rest on the idea of a building, knowing that it represents whatever obscure machinations go on inside.

> **Example 7.1.6**
> The orders came directly from the White House.

The *White House* is associated with the president, but more than that, with all the processes of the executive branch of government. This metonymy, therefore, quite capably expresses the idea that the orders—whether they came from the president's desk personally or from an agent acting on behalf of the president—are the responsibility of the president.

As with all metaphors, the choice of the substitution in a metonymy makes a comment about the subject because the metonymy transfers the qualities of the substitution to the subject. Notice the difference in attitudes toward college conveyed by the choice of substitution in the following metonymies:

> **Example 7.1.7**
> *No metonymy:* After four years of education, I got my bachelor's degree and left college.
> *Neutral metonymy:* After four years of reading and writing, I got my bachelor's degree and left college.
> *Negative metonymy:* After four years of filling in the bubbles on machine-scored answer sheets, I got my bachelor's degree and left college.

Exercise 7.1.1

For each of the following sentences, translate the underlined metonymy into the original subject for which it has been substituted.

(a) It was cool this morning, but look at how <u>the mercury is rising</u> now.

(b) <u>Hollywood</u> is making an ever-increasing use of computer graphics.

Exercise 7.1.2

Revise each sentence, substituting a metonymy (suggested in parentheses) for the underlined subject of the metaphor. Make necessary changes in wording.

    (a) Tomorrow we are going to the <u>zoo</u>. (two animals associated with the zoo)

    (b) They were being watched by a <u>policeman</u>. (something associated with a policeman)

7.2 Synecdoche.

A synecdoche (sin EK duh kē) is also a metaphor of substitution like metonymy. However, rather than substituting something associated with the subject, a part of the subject is substituted for the whole, or the whole for a part. (The substitution can also be the genus for the species, the species for the genus, the material for the thing made, or any other portion for a whole or whole for a portion.) The beatnik slang of the 1950s was rich with synecdoche, as the following example shows.

Example 7.2.1

If I had some wheels, I'd put on my best threads and ask for Jane's hand.

In this example, *wheels* is a part-for-whole substitution for *automobile* (or perhaps *motorcycle*), *threads* is a material-for-thing-made substitution for *clothes*, and *hand* is a part-for-whole substitution for Jane herself.

The part-for-whole substitution is one of the more common forms of synecdoche.

Example 7.2.2

The army includes two hundred horse and three hundred foot. [*horse* substituted for *cavalry soldiers* and *foot* substituted for *foot soldiers*]

Example 7.2.3

It is certainly hard to earn a dollar these days. [*a dollar* substituted for *money*]

Example 7.2.4

Patty's hobby is exposing film; Harold's is burning up gasoline in his dune buggy; Tom's is making sawdust in his workshop. [*exposing film* substituted for *taking pictures*, *burning up gasoline* substituted for *driving*, *making sawdust* substituted for *doing woodwork*]

Example 7.2.5

Okay, team. Get those blades back on the ice. [*blades* substituted for *ice skates*, substituted for the ice hockey players—that is, "Get yourselves back on the ice."]

Whole-for-part substitutions are also possible.

Example 7.2.6

Get in here this instant or I will spank your body. [*body* substituted for *rear end*]

Example 7.2.7

This tree tastes good. [*tree* substituted for *fruit on the tree*]

The substitution of the material for the thing made can produce an effective image.

Example 7.2.8

She grabbed a ceramic from the shelf and poured some coffee. [*ceramic* substituted for a *coffee cup*, which is made of ceramic]

Example 7.2.9

He put the steel to the bolt and turned with all his strength. [*steel* substituted for *wrench*, which is made of steel]

Substituting genus (the more general category or class) for species (the specific type or example) is common, but care should be taken to make the meaning of the substitution clear. Whenever you move to more general from less general, there is the possibility for ambiguity. Usually, you can arrange the context of the use to make the meaning clear.

Example 7.2.10

Captain Ahab hurled the barbed weapon at the whale. [category of *barbed weapon* substituted for *harpoon*]

Example 7.2.11

I'll go get my machine and drive you to the park. [category of *machine* substituted for *automobile*]

Substituting species for genus (that is, a specific example to represent a larger category) is often one of the most effective methods of creating synecdoches, because the increase in specificity adds visual appeal and exactness to the writing.

Example 7.2.12

Those who measure their lives by their possessions have yet to learn that life consists of more than cars and television sets. [two specific items, *cars* and *television sets*, substituted for the idea of material wealth or consumer goods]

Example 7.2.13

This legislation is for the little old lady in Cleveland who cannot afford to pay her heating bill. [one example of a beneficiary substituted for all beneficiaries]

Other kinds of substitution are possible, as well.

Example 7.2.14

A few hundred pounds of twenty-dollar bills ought to solve that problem nicely. [weight substituted for value]

Example 7.2.15

Put Beethoven in the player and turn up the volume. [composer substituted for CD or music]

Synecdoche is sometimes considered a subcategory of metonymy. Some rhetoricians do not distinguish between metonymy and synecdoche because there are often cases in which it is not clear whether the substituted image is a part of the subject (synecdoche) or merely associated with it (metonymy).

Example 7.2.16

I'll make you a sandwich as soon as I wash the dog off my hands.

In the example above, is *dog* a synecdoche (whole for part) for, say, *dog hair*, or is it a metonymy (association) for *dirt and germs* associated with a dog? Or is it both?

Example 7.2.17

Ladies and gentlemen of the jury, this child's blood is on that man's hands.

In the example above, is the metaphor a metonymy (*blood* associated with guilt or the crime) or a synecdoche (*blood* as a part substituting for the entire murder)? In spite of these difficulties, the distinction between synecdoche and metonymy is useful. In the cases of uncertainty like those in Examples 7.2.16 and 7.2.17, calling them metonymies might be the better choice on the grounds that metonymy is the broader term.

Exercise 7.2.1

For each of the following sentences, translate the underlined synecdoche into the original subject for which it has been substituted.

(a) Around here you have to work for your <u>daily bread</u>.

(b) Once again she picked up that <u>technology of interruption</u> and said, "Hello?"

Exercise 7.2.2

Revise each sentence, substituting a synecdoche (suggested in parentheses) for the underlined subject of the metaphor. Make necessary changes in wording.

    (a) It's time for me to stretch out on the <u>bed</u> and take a nap. (one of the materials from which beds are made)

    (b) The workmen spent the day <u>building the dog house for Fido</u>. (one or two specific activities involved in building a dog house)

7.3 Personification.

Personification (pur sahn i fi KĀ shun) metaphorically gives human attributes to animals, objects, or ideas. The human attributes can be those of form, behavior, feelings, attitudes, motivation, and so forth.

Example 7.3.1

The ship began to creak and protest as it struggled against the rising sea.

In this example, ships cannot literally protest or struggle because they are inanimate things. However, personifying the ship here allows the writer to give its actions in the storm qualities that are easy to understand because they are put into human terms.

Because we are so familiar with social relationships, the personification of objects makes our reactions to or interactions with those objects easier to explain.

Example 7.3.2

We bought this house instead of the one on Maple Street because this one is more friendly.

In the example above, describing a house as *friendly* conveys a feeling about the place that might otherwise be difficult to put into words.

Example 7.3.3

This coffee is strong enough to get up and walk away.

Example 7.3.4

I can't get this fuel pump back on because this bolt is being uncooperative.

In this example, the single personification of *uncooperative* immediately makes the situation clear and lifelike, and perhaps better than would a lengthy explanation about how the speaker could not manage to align or thread the bolt properly.

Abstract concepts are frequently personified because by themselves they produce no pictures and are therefore more difficult to process mentally than words that create images. By giving an abstraction human attributes, it is made more concrete and visual and thereby easier to comprehend. To aid the reader in recognizing the personified abstraction, it is usually capitalized.

Example 7.3.5

When they returned from "saving lots of money," Debt began to knock at the door.

Example 7.3.6

The advertising campaign should, of course, highlight the product's strengths; but I don't think we should put a sock in the mouth of Truth, either.

Example 7.3.7

This new code you wrote looks as if it might actually work. At least, it certainly hits Impossible with a big stick.

Occasionally, you may want to use a pronoun (his, her, he, she) when personifying an abstraction. Traditionally, many of the virtues have been personified as women: Justice, Hope, Truth, Love, and Wisdom all have been described as women, probably because of their gender in Greek and Roman mythology. Other abstractions, such as War and Death, have traditionally been personified as men. Newer abstractions might be either male or female. However, whether old or new, be careful not to give offense by gendering the personification of negative abstractions. For example, Discord was traditionally personified as a woman, but to do so today might give offense. Similarly, if you are personifying Disease, Crime, or a similar idea, avoid any gender identification.

Personification is sometimes combined with metonymy to create an interesting metaphorical situation.

Example 7.3.8

I would like to have discussed this further, but my wristwatch is ordering me to leave.

In this example, *wristwatch* is a metonymy for *time*, as well as being personified as someone ordering the speaker to act. Thus, the statement is a polite way of saying that the speaker is out of time and must leave, but is doing so reluctantly, as if being ordered to go by a third person.

Personification of the natural world has traditionally been among the most common types, as seen by expressions such as *lands rejoicing, winds singing, sneering rocks, laughing waves,* and so forth. (This type of personification is sometimes called *fictio.*) Personification involving exaggerated emotionalism has been referred to as the *pathetic fallacy* by

John Ruskin, who considered it to be a vice. Nature stomping around in a frenzy is seldom pretty:

Example 7.3.9
The vicious clouds in the hateful sky cruelly spat down their drops of frozen anger onto the poor traveler who had forgotten his umbrella.

Be careful, then, not to overdo the attributes of emotion in your personifications. At the same time, however, the appropriate use of emotions in personification can often be highly effective. By limiting the emotional description to a word or two, the attributed feelings can appear quite natural.

Example 7.3.10
Even the trees looked frightened by the earthquake.

In the example above, describing trees as looking frightened seems to be a legitimate image because earthquakes shake the trees and their leaves, and we associate trembling with fear. (Saying, "The trees trembled with fear when the earthquake hit," would also work for the same reason.)

Example 7.3.11
After two hours of political platitudes, everyone grew bored. The delegates were bored; the guests were bored; the speaker himself was bored. Even the chairs were bored.

In this example, the idea of bored furniture is highly dramatic. Note that context might be important here because the word *chair* is sometimes used instead of *chairman* or *chairperson*. If the context included people described as *chairs*, the writer would have to use *furniture* or *seats* in the personification instead: *Even the furniture was bored.*

Exercise 7.3.1

For each of the following sentences, fill in the blank with an appropriate personification suggested in parentheses.

(a) Today the computer system _____ at me. (facial expression)

(b) That decision _____. (arrived slowly)

(c) This paragraph _____. (unfocused)

(d) The sixth hole on the golf course was _____. (negative intent)

Style Check 7: Freshness.

As you study the figurative language described in these chapters (6, 7, and 8), keep in mind that such imagery finds its effectiveness by adding striking, visually compelling images to your writing. To be striking, the images should be fresh—either new or at least not overused. Images that have been overused no longer add the attention-getting, thought-clarifying, enjoyment-adding content to the subject at hand. Fresh images add concrete and specific substance to your discussion, while readers no longer even visualize worn-out images. Worn-out images do little more than taint your writing with the odor of cliché.

Many expressions in common overuse began life as interesting images. The first few thousand times they were trotted out, everyone applauded. But now they have become the hobbling old plugs of language, ridden into the ground until they became clichés. Let them retire gracefully, and be fresh and creative with your figurative language.

Below is a table of a handful of metaphors and similes that have turned into clichés, to remind you how tiresome, worn out, and unoriginal they are.

A Sampling of Metaphors and Similes Turned Cliché	
as free as a bird	slept like a log
dead as a doornail	smooth sailing
gentle as a lamb	the bottom line
happy as a clam	the crack of dawn
out like a light	the jaws of defeat
sit on the fence	toot your own horn

Review Questions.

1. For each example, place an *M* in the blank if a metonymy is used, an *S* if a synecdoche is used, and a *P* if personification is used.

_____ When Julie had finished speaking to Tom, it was as if Enlightenment had pulled out her flashlight and shone it in his eyes.

_____ Now that we have agreed on the terms of the contract, we can turn the details over to the suits to draw up the legalese.

_____ That's the third time I've slipped. I don't think this mountain likes me.

_____ After every rain in your heart, may you always find a warm fireside to dry out.

_____ Stop thinking with your stomach. This is more important than lunch.

_____ That guy drives a fast piece of sheet metal.

2. Match the definition with the term.

_____ the substitution of a part for a whole

_____ ascribing human attributes to an object or idea

_____ the substitution of something associated with the subject for the subject itself

A. metonymy

B. synecdoche

C. personification

3. The pathetic fallacy refers to

A. a metonymy that involves logically invalid pathos.

B. a synecdoche that leads the reader along an illogical thinking path.

C. a personification that involves exaggerated emotionalism.

4. Metonymy, synecdoche, and personification are all subtypes of

A. analogy.

B. metaphor.

C. zeugma.

5. For each example, place a C in the blank if the statement contains a cliché and an F in the blank if the statement contains a fresh image.

_____ I need to learn the nuts and bolts of this operation.

_____ This book will help you climb the ladder of success.

_____ You're as organized as a spice rack.

_____ It's time to bite the bullet and accept the write-off.

_____ Problems arrive in fast cars, but they leave on foot.

_____ That film may be a treasure, but it's a dung beetle's treasure.

Chapter 8
Figurative Language III

By these allusions a truth in the understanding is as it were reflected by the imagination; we are able to see something like color and shape in a notion and to discover a scheme of thoughts traced out upon matter.

—Joseph Addison

The proverb, "The more you know, the more you can learn," reminds us that learning is often a process of fitting new ideas into the context of our current knowledge. The figurative language devices in these chapters (6, 7, and 8) enable you to construct associations (or bridges from the familiar to the unfamiliar) that can facilitate your readers' learning process as well as provide aesthetic and imaginative qualities. Thus, these are tools of practical art.

8.1 Allusion.

An allusion (uh LOO zhun) is a short, informal reference to a famous person or event. The allusion often functions as a brief analogy or example to highlight a point being made.

> **Example 8.1.1**
> Plan ahead: It wasn't raining when Noah built the ark. —Richard Cushing

> **Example 8.1.2**
> I think we should do some more risk analysis on this "good idea." After all, Napoleon thought it was a good idea to march on Moscow in the middle of winter.

Allusions are most often drawn from history, Greek and Roman mythology, Shakespeare, the Bible, and literature. Years ago, educated readers were assumed to be familiar with all these areas, so that allusions drawn from them (Pearl Harbor, Sisyphus, Polonius, Job, Gargantua, etc.) would have been familiar, also. Today, however, this knowledge can no longer be assumed, making the construction of allusions more challenging. To be effective, an allusion must have the following qualities:

♦ **Familiarity.** Consider what will be familiar to your particular audience. Teenagers may not know Greek mythology, and retirees may not know those who are famous in popular music. If you are writing to a general audience that might include both teens and older people, you will have to find allusions that all members of the audience are likely to know.

♦ **Endurance.** Consider how long you want your writing to remain accessible to your readers. If you choose an allusion to a current celebrity, the reference might be familiar for only a few years because most celebrities fade and disappear so quickly.

♦ **Focused attribute.** The historical event or person must possess an attribute relevant to your reference. Some famous people are known for several attributes, so you might have to take care to specify which attribute you have in mind.

Example 8.1.3

You must borrow me Gargantua's mouth first. 'Tis a word too great for any mouth of this age's size. —*As You Like It*, 3.2.238

In the example above, Shakespeare supplies information with the allusion to help the reader understand it, even if the name *Gargantua* is not familiar. That Gargantua was a giant is implied by the explanation of the large word requiring a large mouth to pronounce it. The practice of providing clarifying explanation in the course of the reference is a good one.

Example 8.1.4

The staff report concludes that the competition will never move into plastics to meet us head on. But Macbeth thought that a forest could never move against him, either.

Example 8.1.5

But his pet theory is like the bed of Procrustes: He stretches or chops off facts to make sure they always fit.

Example 8.1.6

I think it very remarkable that this House of Commons . . . is ready . . . to accept the perils with which we may be confronted, with a feeling that, God helping, we can do no other. —Winston Churchill

In the example above, Churchill is speaking (in 1939) of England's determination to resist Germany's aggression and of the resulting probability of war with Germany. He alludes to the stand Martin Luther took when he posted his 95 Theses and declared, "Here I stand, I can do no other, so help me God." By echoing Luther's words, Churchill imaginatively links England and Martin Luther in their twin monumental struggles. Luther, by being a German, is cast in the role not so much as a resister of the Catholic Church but as a resister of German authority, so the allusion is especially powerful.

(Note that Churchill's audience would have grasped this allusion immediately: Remember that to be effective, an allusion must be recognized by your audience.)

If you can find the right ones, allusions can be wonderfully attractive in your writing because they can introduce variety and energy into the discussion. An interesting person or exciting event is suddenly recalled, perhaps in the middle of an abstract discussion, creating not only a helpful clarification but also the pleasure of remembering a story.

Exercise 8.1.1

Rewrite the following sentences, substituting the allusion in parentheses for the underlined words. Add words or create a sentence as needed to express the idea clearly.

    (a) This memo came from the boss. That makes these new policies <u>law for us</u>. (the Ten Commandments written on stone tablets)

    (b) When he saw the bill, he gave the table a shake <u>like you wouldn't believe</u>. (the 1994 Northridge earthquake)

8.2 Eponym.

An eponym (EP uh nim) is a specific type of allusion, substituting the name of a person famous for some attribute in place of the attribute itself. The person can be a historical, mythological, literary, or Biblical figure.

Example 8.2.1

This lid is stuck so tight I need a Hercules to open it.

In this example, Hercules is known for his strength, so his name is substituted for *a strong person.*

Eponyms, like other allusions (see Section 8.1 above) should be familiar to your audience in order to be effective. However, many eponyms have been used so often that they border on being cliché, so be careful in your choice. Your eponyms should be familiar but not so familiar that they are trite. (You must steer your choice between the Scylla of unfamiliarity and the Charybdis of cliché, to use an allusion from Homer. They were two monsters on either side of a narrow strait. Getting too close to either would be a disaster: One would eat the ship's crew, and the other would suck the ship under water.)

Example 8.2.2

Is he smart? Why, the man is an Einstein. Is he creative? He's a Leonardo da Vinci. Has he suffered? That poor Job can tell you himself.

Example 8.2.3

Did you see the generous present Scrooge gave his employees this year? A brand new pencil.

Example 8.2.4

Allow me to dispel the confusion that has seized some of our representatives: Uncle Sam is not the same person as Santa Claus.

In cases where the eponym might not be completely familiar to your readers, or where the person is well known for more than one attribute, you should consider adding the intended quality to your description.

Example 8.2.5

The wisdom of Solomon was needed to understand the baffling trends in the appliance marketplace this last quarter.

Example 8.2.6

The Securities Exchange Commission is charged to be the Argus of the stock market: Its hundred eyes are everywhere.

In these examples, Solomon's characteristic (wisdom) and Argus' characteristic (having a hundred eyes) are mentioned in the course of using the eponym so that the reference becomes clear, even for a reader who does not recognize the name or its attribute.

Exercise 8.2.1

Rewrite the following sentences, substituting the eponym in parentheses for the underlined words. Add words or create a sentence as needed to express the idea clearly.

   (a) We need a fund manager with <u>an eye for the best stocks</u>. (touch of Midas)
   (b) Many magazines today splash <u>a beautiful woman</u> on the cover to increase sales. (Helen of Troy)

8.3 Apostrophe.

An apostrophe (uh POS truh fē) is a direct address to someone, whether present or absent, and whether real, imaginary, or personified. Its most common purpose is to permit the writer to turn away from the subject under discussion for a moment and give expression to built-up emotion. In the example below, Richard de Bury interrupts his praise of books to talk to books themselves:

Example 8.3.1

O books who alone are liberal and free, who give to all who ask of you and enfranchise all who serve you faithfully! —Richard de Bury

As the example above shows, apostrophe often appears together with personification because the subject of the address is often a humanized thing or abstraction. The address to a personified abstraction is the most common form of apostrophe found in literary works.

Because of its emotional departure from reasoned discourse, apostrophe is rare in formal prose, but it still can be effective under the right circumstances, especially in semiformal writing. Once again, consider your subject and audience to determine what is appropriate.

Example 8.3.2

After this last piece of unexpected news, the stock collapsed completely, ending its fall from $84 a share a year earlier to less than a dollar now. You poor shareholders! If only you had known about those secret partnerships! How much wiser you could have been!

Breaking the stream of discourse to address the reader directly enables the writer to make a personal comment.

Example 8.3.3

The winds died down and the chain saws came out to remove the fallen trees. The city said the entire cost of the storm was under $50,000. But how, dear reader, will we ever put a number on the loss of those beautiful old oak and olive trees?

A brief apostrophe can be inserted parenthetically (see the discussion of parenthesis in Chapter 10, Section 10.4).

Example 8.3.4

The fact that a bag of fertilizer and a can of fuel oil can be made into a bomb reminds us that—sorry to give you the bad news—many everyday items can become the weapons of terrorists.

Example 8.3.5

In spite of regular articles criticizing the empty calories of junk food eaten during television watching, billions of dollars are spent annually on chips and dips, which are so beloved that they have now been even further exalted by the name of *comfort foods*. (How weak by comparison, oh Healthy Snacks, are *your* blandishments!)

Exercise 8.3.1

After each of the following sentences, add an apostrophe suggested by the parenthetical comment. Add words as needed to express the idea clearly.

    (a) Next week I'm going to the dentist. (Address your teeth and feel sorry for them.)

    (b) The winter deepened and the snows came. (Address the snow and tell it you love it.)

8.4 Transferred Epithet.

An ordinary epithet (EP uh thet) is an adjective or adjective phrase that describes a key characteristic of the noun. The table below offers a few examples.

Example Epithets	
brightening dawn	peaceful sunset
cruel murder	sneering contempt
laughing happiness	untroubled sleep

Epithets can also be metaphorical, usually with personified characteristics, as the examples in the table below demonstrate.

Example Metaphorical Epithets	
joyous firefly	smirking billboards
lazy road	tired landscape
sleeping night	wandering river

A **transferred epithet** is an adjective modifying a noun that it cannot normally modify, but that makes figurative sense.

> **Example 8.4.1**
>
> At length I heard a ragged noise and mirth of thieves and murderers. . . .
> —George Herbert

In the example above, the word *ragged* cannot normally modify *noise* because *ragged* refers to the rough edge of something physical such as cloth or wood. However, the image is highly effective because the reader senses that the noise is of a kind that stems from a rabble (thieves and murderers) making a noise metaphorically akin to a ragged edge.

Example 8.4.2

In an age of pressurized happiness, we sometimes grow insensitive to subtle joys.

Example 8.4.3

Just as the meeting was about to adjourn, she asked a sandy question that left grit in everyone's teeth.

Example 8.4.4

His preference for bright colors explains why he always wears such clattering shirts.

In the example above, the use of *clattering* (an adjective of sound) for a shirt is easily understood because the transferred epithet *loud* is already commonly used to describe bright colors: *He's wearing a loud shirt*.

Sometimes the meaning of the transferred epithet is made clearer because of the traditional metaphorical associations connected with the adjective.

Example 8.4.5

The mind . . . creates . . .
Far other worlds, and other seas,
Annihilating all that's made
To a green thought in a green shade.
—Andrew Marvell

In this example, Marvell uses the adjective *green* in the transferred epithet *green thought* to draw upon the traditional metaphorical meanings of greenness: life, growth, creativity, prosperity, youth. On the other hand, saying, "I had a purple thought yesterday," would not produce a similar understanding in the reader because the symbolic meanings of purple are not as familiar to most readers.

If you think that your reader may not understand the meaning of your transferred epithet, you can combine it with scesis onomaton (see Chapter 13, Section 13.4) and supply one or more synonymous expressions.

Example 8.4.6

How many summers must pass while this constant brownout, this low voltage, this diluted electricity continues to harm our appliances?

In the example above, the transferred epithet *diluted electricity* is made clear by its connection with *brownout* and *low voltage*.

Many instances of catachresis (see Chapter 6, Section 6.4), such as Milton's *blind mouths*, consist of transferred epithets because the epithets make such striking metaphors. Indeed, a transferred epithet is so striking and memorable that repeating it might create the appearance of obvious cleverness, an action almost guaranteed to distance your reader. If you discuss a subject at length or have several synonyms (as in Example 8.4.6 above), the most effective approach is to use the transferred epithet once and place it last, where it will stand out as your culminating, surprising characterization.

Exercise 8.4.1

Choose an adjective from the left column and a noun from the right column to form a transferred epithet. Then write a sentence containing the epithet. Do this twice, for a total of two sentences. If necessary, supply language that makes the meaning clear.

Adjectives	Nouns
dusty	contract
humid	gift
leafy	motion picture
oily	speech
smoggy	thought

Style Check 8: Persona.

Persona refers to the personality that a writer reveals (or creates) through the writing. Aspects of persona include how knowledgeable the writer appears, what beliefs and values guide the writing, how calm or emotional the writer is, and so forth.

All writing reflects a persona: Even writers who take care to remove themselves from their writing as far as possible still reveal a persona to their readers. The persona behind much academic and scientific writing often appears to be detached, emotionless, cerebral, and guarded. Unfortunately, to some audiences such a persona may be perceived as cold, passionless, and even dull. Therefore, a single persona for all purposes will not be the most effective strategy to adopt.

Depending on your audience and your subject matter, you can choose the persona you want to reflect in your writing: how formal or informal, warm or cold, friendly or aloof, thoughtful or witty, and so forth. For a particular project, you may want to adopt a persona that is more scientific, reasoned, and detailed than your natural style would reveal. For another project, you might want to be more personal and friendly than you might be otherwise.

In short, as you write, think about how you appear to your readers as the person behind the ideas. Present yourself (through your attitude, your vocabulary, and your other writing choices—including the use of rhetorical devices) in a way that will encourage your readers to put confidence in you.

Review Questions.

1. Match the rhetorical device with the appropriate example.
   _____ Thank you, O trees, for giving me a shady place to nap.
   _____ There goes Amy with another armful of blankets. She's a real Mother Theresa.
   _____ Are you still driving around on those slithering tires?
   _____ Your paperwork is done? Now you know what it feels like to climb to the top of Mount Everest.
   A. allusion
   B. eponym
   C. apostrophe
   D. transferred epithet

2. Match the device with the question.
   _____ Which device allows you to address the reader directly?
   _____ Which device allows you to bring in a famous historical event?
   _____ Which device creates a seemingly illogical image with metaphorical meaning?
   _____ Which device substitutes a famous person's name for a characteristic?
   A. allusion
   B. eponym
   C. apostrophe
   D. transferred epithet

3. Which is an example of a transferred epithet?
   A. winding road
   B. dangerous road
   C. dusty road
   D. tea-drinking road

4. Which solution is most effective for clarification if the meaning of a transferred epithet is not clear by itself?
   A. add a metaphor
   B. include a string of synonyms (scesis onomaton)
   C. construct a synecdoche
   D. ask a rhetorical question

5. The persona of an essay refers to
   A. how the writer perceives himself or herself.
   B. how the reader perceives the personality of the writer.
   C. the writer's actual personality.

Notes

Chapter 9
Syntax I

My goal will be a comfortable style that seems easy enough for anyone to write—but those who try will sweat and strive in vain. The secret lies in the careful arrangement that adds strength and beauty to the familiar.
—Horace, *The Art of Poetry*

The term *syntax* refers to the way words and phrases are put together to form sentences. This chapter presents several devices that employ particular arrangements of and relationships between words—in other words, devices involving syntactical structures. These devices can add substantially to your writing style, by producing a sense of clean, organized, and clear information.

9.1 Zeugma.

Zeugma (ZOOG muh) and its related forms (see the several devices following) all involve linking together two or more words, phrases, or clauses by another word that is stated in one place and only implied in the rest of the sentence. The simplest example is the use of one verb to link two subjects, as in the following example, where *Jane* and *Tom* share the verb *jogged*:

Example 9.1.1
Jane and Tom jogged along the trail together.

You most likely already use zeugma like this. Similarly, you may already sometimes write a sentence with one verb and two or more direct objects. In the example below, the verb *grabbed* is implied in front of *her gloves* and *her car keys*.

Example 9.1.2
She grabbed her purse from the alcove, her gloves from the table near the door, and her car keys from the punchbowl.

Zeugma can involve the linking of any words (any parts of speech), not just verbs. An instance would be a preposition with two objects. In the example below, the preposition *of* is implied in front of *the whole conference*.

Example 9.1.3

The most significant part of the speech and the whole conference was the call for more standardized sentencing guidelines.

Linking multiple words or phrases through an implied word enables the writer to show clear relationships and produces a smooth and flowing sentence. In the examples presented above, the linking is standard writing practice because it has the additional benefit of reducing wordiness: Repeating the verb *grabbed* in Example 9.1.2, for instance, would seem redundant, if not awkward.

The devices that follow in this chapter are all subcategories of zeugma. For linkages that do not fit into one of the categories below, use the general term *zeugma*. The discussion of climax in Chapter 2, Section 2.1, includes examples that also contain zeugma.

Exercise 9.1.1

Revise each of these sentences by removing the repeated subjects and verbs to create a zeugmatic construction.

Example sentence: The emperor built a castle. He built a park. Then he built a hunting lodge.
Example revision: The emperor built a castle, a park, and a hunting lodge.

(a) The workman drilled into the base rock, and he drilled through the rock wall.
(b) The people voted for more limits on government, but they voted for more services, too.

9.2 Diazeugma.

Diazeugma (dī uh ZOOG muh) consists of a single subject linking multiple verbs or verb phrases. The phrases are usually put into parallel form to make the sentence easier to follow and to give it a balanced feel. In the example below, the word *book* links the verb phrases beginning with *reveals*, *discusses*, and *argues*.

Example 9.2.1

The book reveals the extent of counterintelligence operations, discusses the options for improving security, and argues for an increase in human intelligence measures.

In the example below, the subject *argument* links the verbs *began* and *ended*, with the material presented not only in parallel but also in antithetical form, stressing the contrast between disputing and fighting.

Example 9.2.2

The argument began in a dispute over the meaning of a word and ended in a fight over the ownership of ten thousand acres.

It is usually best to restrict diazeugma to two or three linkages. If there are three, keeping them short is probably more effective than allowing them to be longer.

Example 9.2.3

The cat rolled on her back, raised her paws, and clawed the air.

Three or more long linkages might call attention to themselves and give the reader a sense of too much art. Remember the saying, "Great art hides art." If your readers cease to pay attention to the meaning and get caught up in the rhetoric, the communication has been diminished.

Exercise 9.2.1

Revise each of these sentences by removing the repeated subjects to create a diazeugmatic construction.

(a) The spotlight slipped from the mounting, and it crashed to the floor.

(b) To create the wallpaper, the artist copied the shapes of diatoms. She colored the shapes with bright paints. Then she assembled the pictures randomly.

9.3 Prozeugma.

In prozeugma (prō ZOOG muh), the linking word is presented once and then omitted from the subsequent sets of words or phrases linked together. The linking word is often a verb. In the following example, the verb *excelled* is stated in the first clause and then implied in the subsequent clauses.

Example 9.3.1

The freshman excelled in calculus; the sophomore, in music; the senior, in drama.

Nearly any verb can be implied:

Example 9.3.2

For travel, the automobile provides the freedom to wander; the train, the convenience of inattentiveness to the journey; and flying, the fastest way home.

Prozeugma is sometimes chosen for the presentation of ideas when the verb itself is less important than the other information in the sentence. Forms of the *to be* verb (*is, are,* and so forth) are good candidates for prozeugmatic omission, as are linking verbs (*seem, appear, remain, feel,* and so forth). Both types of verb can be easily implied in a sequence of clauses.

Example 9.3.3
During the concert, Fred will be in the sound booth, Jane at the light board, and Tim behind the curtain.

Exercise 9.3.1
Revise each of these sentences by removing the repeated verbs to create a prozeugmatic construction.
(a) The digital copier reduces the need for printed originals; e-mail reduces the need for hardcopy memos; and the Web reduces the need for printed articles.
(b) Heraclitus argued that you cannot step into the same river twice, and Zeno argued that you will never arrive at the river in the first place.

9.4 Mesozeugma.

With mesozeugma (mez uh ZOOG muh), the linking word (often a verb) comes in the middle of the sentence. In the example below, the linking words are *is included*, connecting *a center speaker* at the beginning of the sentence and *a subwoofer* at the end. Note that removing the verb in the second part of the sentence shifts the emphasis from the verb idea (*included*) to the object of inclusion (*subwoofer*).

Example 9.4.1
A center speaker is included, and a subwoofer.

In the example above and in the two examples that follow, the linking word is part of the first half of the sentence (the first clause). In the examples below, *the blouse was creased* forms a complete sentence, as does *the radio test worked perfectly*.

Example 9.4.2
The blouse was creased but not the scarf.

Example 9.4.3
The radio test worked perfectly, and the telemetry check.

Each use of mesozeugma should be analyzed by your sense of art and taste for the effect it creates. In Example 9.4.2 above, the use appears natural and effective for formal prose. The use in Example 9.4.3 creates the sense of an afterthought, as if the sentence represents a spontaneous or conversational comment. Such a usage would be best in fiction or informal prose.

Alternative to placing the linking word in the first clause, it can be placed in the subsequent clause. Note in the example below that the first part of the sentence, *either the truth,* is now missing the verb, which has been placed in the second part of the sentence, *say nothing at all.*

Example 9.4.4

Either the truth or say nothing at all. —Adapted from George Puttenham

---

Exercise 9.4.1

Revise each of these sentences by placing one of the parallel elements after the verb to create a mesozeugmatic construction.

(a) The governor and then the reporter left the news conference.

(b) The intended benefits but not the unintended costs of the bill were considered.

9.5 Hypozeugma.

In hypozeugma (hī pō ZOOG muh), the linking word follows the words it links together. A common form is the presentation of multiple subjects.

Example 9.5.1

Monkeys, giraffes, elephants, and even lions had escaped from the zoo after the earthquake.

Example 9.5.2

Producing 400 megawatts and achieving a reliability of 99 percent will require a completely new generator design.

Hypozeugma can be used to create a periodic sentence (see the Style Check at the end of this chapter), holding off the verb until the last clause and thereby requiring the reader to pay close attention to the sentence, as in the example below.

Example 9.5.3

The crying infant from its crib, the desperate woman off the roof, and the injured man from the flooded basement were all rescued.

The linking word can be a noun, with the linked words consisting of modifiers, as in the following example, where the noun *researchers* is modified by two extended adjective phrases.

Example 9.5.4

Encouraged by the success of the early tests and looking forward to the new grant money, the researchers projected an unusual air of confidence.

Exercise 9.5.1

Revise each of these sentences by moving the underlined words to the end of the sentence to create a hypozeugmatic construction.

  (a) <u>The new cruise ships are designed to be like cities</u>, purifying their own water, processing their own waste, and generating their own electricity.
  (b) <u>Features made of stone are</u> the roadway, the bridge, and the hotel.

9.6 Syllepsis.

Syllepsis (si LEP sis) is a device similar to ordinary zeugma, except that the terms are linked (almost always by a verb) in different senses or meanings of the linking word. The example below will clarify this.

Example 9.6.1

She was unwilling to drive to that party because she was afraid to damage her car or her reputation.

Here, of course, a car is damaged in a way different from the way a reputation is damaged, so the meaning of *damage* must change senses in mid-sentence.

Sometimes the different senses of the linking word include a literal sense and a figurative sense, as in the following examples.

Example 9.6.2

He grabbed his hat from the rack by the door and a kiss from the lips of his wife.

In the example above, a hat is quite literally grabbed with a hand, while a kiss is more figuratively grabbed (quickly taken) with the lips.

In the next example, the syllepsis hinges on a change in meaning of the verb *lost*. A heart is lost figuratively, while money is lost literally.

Example 9.6.3

As a result of the whirlwind romance, she lost her heart and her savings to the confidence man.

On the other hand, the two senses of the verb often both involve somewhat different literal meanings, as in the example below.

Example 9.6.4

Seething with anger, he shut his mouth and the door. Then he smashed the clock into pieces and his fist through the wall.

In this example, shutting one's mouth and shutting a door both involve literal meanings of *shut*, but in slightly different senses. Similarly, smashing a clock includes the idea of destroying it, while smashing a fist through a door refers more to the force of the blow.

Syllepsis is primarily a device of wit. The incongruity perceived by the need to change senses of the linking word produces a humorous, witty effect for the reader. If the examples above were effective, you should have felt a smile as you read them.

Exercise 9.6.1

Revise each of these sentences by removing the repeated word to create syllepsis.
  (a) When daylight saving time ends, change your clocks, change your smoke alarm batteries, and change your mind about sleeping late.
  (b) He liked the coffee shop in the bookstore because in one place he could feed his mind and feed his stomach.

Style Check 9: Cumulative and Periodic Sentences.

Two important methods for structuring the presentation of ideas in a sentence are the cumulative and the periodic. A cumulative sentence presents the main idea first and then adds modification, detail, and qualification afterwards.

Style Check Example 9.1

The joint leaked after the third pressure test at low temperature and high vibration.

In this example, *the joint leaked* presents the main idea. The words following supply detail.

Most sentences are at least roughly cumulative because the cumulative structure produces sentences that are easy to understand and follow. Cumulative sentences feel natural and familiar to readers. The two drawbacks are first, that hurried readers may skip much of the sentence once they get the main idea, and second, that cumulative sentences have no natural stopping point:

They are open ended and could conceivably run on and on. Note in the following example that the sentence (or the reader) could stop at any of the points marked by the vertical bar (|) and still have the sense of a complete idea with some detail.

Style Check Example 9.2

Apply the fertilizer | every month | using a spreader | from the fertilizer maker | spraying at a medium rate | which is one ounce per 100 square feet | except in the fall | when the rate can be increased | to about three ounces per 100 square feet. |

A periodic sentence, on the other hand, presents modification first or in some other way holds off the completion of the main idea until the very end. The simplest example of a periodic sentence is one with an introductory subordinate clause, as in the following example.

Style Check Example 9.3

When students knew they were being observed, they scored less well on the test.

More elaborate periodic sentences are possible by supplying various kinds of modification in front of the main idea.

Style Check Example 9.4

Having gathered mushrooms from his own hothouse, personally selected the spinach leaves from the window-box garden, and chopped the ham and cheese, the Saturday chef made himself an omelet.

Style Check Example 9.5

From her seat across the garden and shaded by the trees, the Queen, still too young to worry about policy or strict propriety, thinking now only of listening to her own heart, and having fixed her eyes on the Count as he served the ball to his eager-eyed opponent, clapped and yelled, "Bravo" as the ball sped over the net.

In the example above, the full meaning of the sentence is not clear until the verb *clapped* appears near the end. Only then is the core sentence (*the Queen clapped*) revealed.

Examples 9.5.3 and 9.5.4 of hypozeugma in Section 9.5 above are periodic in structure because the main idea (either the verb or the entire main clause) is held off until the end of the sentence.

Because the meaning of a periodic sentence is not completely clear until the sentence ends, periodic sentences are more difficult to read than standard cumulative sentences. Periodic sentences force the reader to pay close attention and to remember the elements read at first, while waiting for the verb or completion of the idea. Forcing the reader to pay attention is a powerful way to emphasize information.

In a word, then, use an occasional periodic sentence structure for emphasis by placing it among your usual cumulative sentences.

Review Questions.

1. Match the type of zeugma with the example in each case.

_____ This fabric feels like nylon; but that one, like silk.

_____ The wings of butterflies, the feathers of birds, and the skins of snakes filled the display cases.

_____ The restaurant closed and then the store.

_____ Captain Jim picked up the typewriter, tied the rope around it, and threw it overboard to anchor his boat.

A. diazeugma

B. prozeugma

C. mesozeugma

D. hypozeugma

2. For each example, place an *S* in the blank if the verb usage represents syllepsis (the verb must be understood in different senses) or *Z* if the verb usage represents ordinary zeugma (the verb can be understood in the same sense).

_____ Last summer the lake and his water ski business dried up.

_____ When he staggered in from the fight, she patched up his wounds and his feelings.

_____ In the library, they could locate neither the book nor the photograph.

3. For each example, place a *C* in the blank if the sentence is cumulative or a *P* if it is periodic.

_____ Popular music, commercial movies, personal photographs, computer software, and file backups of many kinds are all uses for compact discs.

_____ The fountain is run by a computer that controls lights, nozzle direction, spray height, and music volume.

_____ Wolf is the dog that has matured faster and become more responsible than naughty little Bear.

_____ If an inflation clause can be included and if the payments can be sheltered from exchange-rate fluctuation, then I think we can approve the contract.

4. Which of the following is **not** one of the effects of using the zeugmatic devices?

A. showing a clear relationship between ideas

B. creating smoothness and flow in a sentence

C. conveying ironic meaning

Notes

Chapter 10
Syntax II

But true expression, like th' unchanging sun,
Clears and improves whate'er it shines upon.
—Alexander Pope, *Essay on Criticism*

English syntax is enormously flexible and pliable. A given set of words can be assembled in numerous ways. (You may have played word games such as "move the adverb" in your grammar classes.) Having several alternative ways to arrange your ideas in a sentence empowers you to choose the focus of attention, to improve the rhythm of your prose, and to impact the artistic effects of the writing overall, even when you are writing professional or business documents. This chapter provides several more ways to direct your readers' attention and interest by using unusual syntax.

10.1 Hyperbaton.

Hyperbaton (hī PUR buh tahn) refers to any departure from normal word order. The unexpected arrangement of words calls sharp attention to the word or words that are out of their usually expected place, thus emphasizing them. Displacing a word to the end or beginning of the sentence (the positions of greatest emphasis) further stresses them, as seen in the two examples below.

> **Example 10.1.1**
> Disturb me not!

> **Example 10.1.2**
> Books they have demanded and books they will get.

The normal expression for Example 10.1.1 would be, "Do not disturb me." The irregular order of words in the hyperbaton, together with the position of *not* at the end of the sentence, creates a strong effect. Similarly, *books* receives emphasis because the word is placed both out of proper sequence (which would be, "They have demanded books") and at the beginning of each clause.

One way to create a hyperbatonic sentence is to flip it around.

> **Example 10.1.3**
> *Normal word order:* You should attend first those who need medicine.
> *Hyperbatonic order (flipped):* Those who need medicine you should attend first.

Another way to make use of hyperbaton is to insert a phrase or clause between the subject and verb of a standard sentence, as in the following example.

Example 10.1.4
> *Normal word order:* After all the pressure against it, the law prevailed.
> *Hyperbatonic order (inserted):* The law, after all the pressure against it, prevailed.

The devices that follow in this chapter are all subcategories of hyperbaton. For unusual syntax that does not fit into one of the categories below, use the general term *hyperbaton*.

Exercise 10.1.1

Rewrite the following sentences, changing the normal word order of the sentences into a word order that uses hyperbaton. Follow the model example in parentheses.
   (a) I like chocolate and I will eat chocolate. (See Example 10.1.2.)
   (b) Because of an error in the contract, the film rights to the novel were lost. (See Example 10.1.4.)

10.2 Anastrophe.

Anastrophe (uh NAS trō fē) involves the reversal or transposition of words. A common form involves placing an adjective behind the noun it modifies instead of in front of it. The usual effect is to emphasize the adjective because it now becomes the last word in the sentence or clause. Such a construction is useful when the adjective is more important than the noun.

Example 10.2.1
> *Normal word order:* His was a sad countenance.
> *Anastrophe:* His was a countenance sad.

When the modification is especially lengthy, putting it behind the noun prevents an awkward sentence.

Example 10.2.2
> *Adjective phrase in front:* She had an indescribable-by-any-words-I-know personality.
> *Anastrophe:* She had a personality indescribable by any words I know.

If you want to amplify the adjective, putting it after the noun allows an effective repetition (see anadiplosis, Chapter 12, Section 12.1, and amplification, Chapter 5, Section 5.3).

Example 10.2.3

From his seat on the bench, he saw the girl content—content with the promise that she could ride on the train again next week.

When you put the adjective behind the noun, especially when the adjective is a single word, always test it for effectiveness (using your sense of taste or by asking others). Otherwise, the resulting expression might appear bizarre, affected, or silly, like the ones in the following example.

Example 10.2.4

Welcome to our home comfortable.
She displayed an air of confidence unusual.
That is a story amazing.

The expressions in the example above may all produce a wince by your reader and red ink by your editor or instructor. Note, however, that a longer adjective phrase is often more acceptable. The above expressions can be revised into quite acceptable prose by the addition of another adjective, as in the following example.

Example 10.2.5

Welcome to our home, comfortable and relaxing.
She displayed an air of confidence unusual for someone so young.
That is a story amazing but true.

Anastrophe can also be constructed by separating two adjectives by the noun they modify, creating a construction similar to mesozeugma (See Chapter 9, Section 9.4).

Example 10.2.6

Normal word order: It was a long but successful operation.
Anastrophe: It was a long operation but successful.

Example 10.2.7

Normal word order: Let's go on a cooler and less busy day.
Anastrophe: Let's go on a cooler day and less busy.

Example 10.2.8

Normal word order: The fitting will require a larger, one-inch-diameter bolt.
Anastrophe: The fitting will require a larger bolt, one inch in diameter.

Once again, the effect is not only to provide some variety in your writing but also to focus attention on the second adjective, which now ends the sentence. There is also some flavor of spontaneity, as a second, seemingly unplanned adjective is apparently added as an afterthought. The resulting freshness is usually welcome.

Exercise 10.2.1

Rewrite the following sentences, changing the normal word order of the underlined adjectives and nouns into the word order of anastrophe.

    (a) She sang with an <u>unrestrained voice</u>.
    (b) These are <u>valuable and carefully performed experiments</u>.
    (c) Mr. Perkins required <u>a dangerous but necessary operation</u>.

10.3 Appositive.

An appositive (uh POZ uh tiv) is a noun that redescribes another noun standing next to it. The two nouns are in apposition (not opposition) to each other.

Example 10.3.1

    Mrs. Wilkins, the manager, told me about the plans for expansion.

In this example, the noun *Mrs. Wilkins* is redescribed by another noun, *manager*. The appositive provides additional information about the original noun. Appositives may involve more than simple nouns, however. Note the modification added to the appositive in the following example, where noun phrases are used:

Example 10.3.2

    The ability to grade coins, a skill requiring experience as well as knowledge,
    cannot be learned overnight from a textbook.

Here, *the ability to grade coins* is a noun phrase, and *a skill requiring experience as well as knowledge* is another noun phrase, standing in apposition to the first one.

The use of appositives is commonly taught as a renaming of the subject, as in the examples above. In such cases, the subject of the sentence is named, the sentence is interrupted by the appositive, and then the sentence continues with the verb and other elements. The typical set-off is achieved with commas.

However, appositives are much more flexible than that. First, other punctuation, such as dashes or parentheses, can be used.

Example 10.3.3

The last cookie—a gingerbread man with one leg—was left on the plate after the party.

Example 10.3.4

The *Hoku Maru* (a Japanese freighter berthed nearby) will require both cranes for unloading.

Instead of following the subject, the appositive can be placed in front of the subject noun it modifies.

Example 10.3.5

A traditional feast of six-foot sandwiches and chips, the picnic was always well attended.

In fact, not just a noun used as a subject, but any noun can take an appositive. For example, an appositive can be placed after a noun at the end of a sentence.

Example 10.3.6

The firm's work on the virus code was interrupted by an unexpected event, a power failure.

In this example, once again, a dash, parentheses, or a colon could be used to set off the appositive. Notice also that appositives are often more effective when they add detail to a more general noun. In Example 10.3.3, *cookie* is detailed as *a gingerbread man*; and in Example 10.3.6, *unexpected event* is detailed as *a power failure*.

Exercise 10.3.1

Underline the appositive word or phrase in each of the following sentences.

(a) That afternoon, Mom showed the kids a new game: raking leaves.

(b) The red manual, an outline of steps to take in an emergency, should be kept within easy reach.

(c) A product of robotic manufacturing, the fan had been made at night in the dark after the plant workers had gone home.

Exercise 10.3.2

Write three sentences, each containing an appositive, according to these instructions.

(a) Put the appositive at the beginning of the sentence, as in Example 10.3.5.

(b) Put the appositive in the middle of the sentence, as in Example 10.3.2.

(c) Put the appositive at the end of the sentence, as in Example 10.3.6.

10.4 Parenthesis.

Parenthesis (puh REN thuh sis) consists of a word, phrase, or entire sentence inserted as an aside into the middle of another sentence.

Example 10.4.1

But the new calculations—and here we see the value of relying on up-to-date information—showed that man-powered flight was possible with this design.

The verbal violence involved in stopping one sentence in order to jump in and present some other information grabs the reader's attention in a dramatic way. It creates the sense that the writer could not wait even until the next sentence to make an announcement relevant to the current idea. The emphasis of the interruption is most profound when dashes are used and when the interruption consists of an entire sentence.

Example 10.4.2

The collection of vases was not inventoried—remember this was the priceless Stimson collection—until four months after the suspected break-in.

The interruption can be less than a sentence, of course.

Example 10.4.3

The ship's crew—after three days at sea in a raft—reached the coast of St. Thomas.

To set off the parenthetical interruption less dramatically, commas can be used.

Example 10.4.4

An enciphered code, like the one used in the cablegrams decrypted in the FBI's Venona project, can be theoretically unbreakable.

The least emphatic way of setting off a parenthetical interruption is with the use of parentheses.

Example 10.4.5

The volume of candle products (including scented waxes and gels) is expected to increase 20 percent this year.

Whether consisting of a dramatic dashed sentence interruption or a more modest parenthetical phrase, the use of parenthesis confers a natural, spoken, informal feel to a sentence. Many speakers interrupt themselves just this way, so similar interruptions in writing give the prose a feel of having been spoken. As with periodic sentences (see Chapter 9, Style Check 9), sentences with lengthy parenthetical constructions demand the reader's careful attention in order to be fully understood. The first part of the inter-

rupted sentence must be held in mind, suspended, while the parenthetical rema
processed. Thus, parenthesis is a good choice for occasions when you want your r
to pay particular attention, and yet feel a sense of spontaneity in your thought proce

---

Exercise 10.4.1

For each case below, insert the underlined words parenthetically into the sentence in a logical place. Use commas, parentheses, or dashes, as you choose.

(a) The use of edge enhancement made the photographs much clearer. <u>an image-sharpening process</u>

(b) Swimmers should be careful to avoid the area where the jellyfish are located. <u>Parents please watch your children.</u>

(c) Applying the factory-recommended torque is essential to prevent either a loose fitting or a broken bolt. <u>Check the manual.</u>

Style Check 10: Parataxis and Hypotaxis.

Parataxis (par uh TAK sis) consists of combining several sentences (that is, independent clauses) with coordinating conjunctions. The seven coordinating conjunctions are *and, or, nor, for, but, so,* and *yet.* Hypotaxis (hī pō TAK sis) is the use of subordination to show a logical relationship between sentences (or ideas). Parataxis and coordinating conjunctions present sentences of equal importance, while hypotaxis presents one sentence (the main or independent clause) as more important than the other (the subordinate clause). Compare the difference:

Style Check Example 10.1

Parataxis: The curtain opened on a brightly painted cartoon set, and the actors entered the stage in vivid costumes.

Hypotaxis: After the curtain opened on a brightly painted cartoon set, the actors entered the stage in vivid costumes.

In the example above, using parataxis gives equal importance to the curtains opening and the actors entering. The hypotactic example presents the actors entering as more important because that idea is presented in a main clause while the curtains opening are placed in a subordinate clause.

Style Check Example 10.2

Parataxis: The rangers measured the rainfall depth in the beaker, but the anemometer was broken, so no wind-speed data were available.

Hypotaxis: Although the rangers measured the rainfall depth in the beaker, no wind-speed data were available because the anemometer was broken.

In this example, paratactic presentation creates an equality among the three ideas. The hypotactic example clearly shows that the lack of wind-speed data is the most important idea of the three because it alone is presented in an independent clause.

Parataxis makes for a simpler sentence structure, even with very long sentences. A good example is Jonathan Swift's *Gulliver's Travels*. In that book, Swift uses an average sentence length of about thirty-eight words, with some sentences as long as sixty words. Yet the book is commonly assigned to junior high and high school students because it is easy to understand. The reason is that Swift uses parataxis extensively, effectively breaking up lengthy sentences into smaller, independent units. For narrative or description, or whenever many ideas of equal importance are to be presented, parataxis is an effective sentence structure.

Hypotaxis permits the writer to show the logical relationships between ideas, one idea depending upon another or related to another in some way. Most important, it allows the writer to reveal which ideas are more important than others, and how the other ideas support the more important ideas. Note in the table of subordinating conjunctions below that relationships of time, reason, and condition can be expressed between ideas by using hypotaxis. Hypotaxis is especially useful for explanation and persuasion, where logical connections between ideas make the discussion clearer.

Example Subordinating Conjunctions

Time	Reason	Concession	Place	Condition	Manner
after	because	although	where	assuming that	as if
before	in order that	even though	wherever	if	as though
since	since	while		in case	how
until	so that			provided that	
when	why			unless	
whenever				until	
while					

Style Check Exercise 10.1

For each case below, change the parataxis into hypotaxis. See Style Check Examples 10.1 and 10.2 above. You may choose subordinating conjunctions from the table above.

    (a) The reporters were curious about the paint spill, so they asked about its source.

    (b) One of the generators broke down, and the cruise ship lost half its power.

    (c) Freeways have been built for decades now, but the architecture of overpasses has changed little.

Style Check Exercise 10.2

For each case below, change the hypotaxis into parataxis. See Style Check Examples 10.1 and 10.2 above. Remember to use one of the seven coordinating conjunctions: *and, or, nor, for, but, so, yet.*

     (a) After the divers swam to the coral reef, they photographed the larger formations.

     (b) Although George I was king of England, he spoke German, not English.

     (c) Research and development are important because new products are our future.

Review Questions.

1. Match the type of hyperbaton with the example in each case.

    _____ Exploring below a few hundred feet—submarines have been crushed by the pressure there—will require a different design from that of our current robot camera.

    _____ *Outlandish Proverbs* is a collection made by George Herbert, a seventeenth-century poet.

    _____ In the corner, the paramedics saw the child shivering.

A. anastrophe

B. appositive

C. parenthesis

2. For each example, place an *A* in the blank if the sentence contains anastrophe or an *N* if the sentence does not.

    _____ His is an idea similar to yours.

    _____ We are looking for a light gold or warm orange paint color.

    _____ The music of Albinoni puts me into a serious mood and somewhat thoughtful.

3. For each example, place a *P* in the blank if the sentence exhibits parataxis or an *H* if it exhibits hypotaxis.

    _____ The trucks need to be packed with supplies, and the medical personnel must be briefed, but the drivers do not have to know the route yet.

    _____ The tumor can be imaged by a CAT scan, or we can simply take some regular X-rays.

    _____ The Hawaiian card company printed the cards on the mainland because shipping them in cargo containers was inexpensive.

    _____ Until individuals were personally asked for help, they walked on by the accident victims.

4. Which is true of an appositive?
    A. It is a noun that restates another noun.
    B. It always follows the noun it restates.
    C. It can restate nouns other than the subject.
    D. Only choices A and C are correct.

5. Which is the most dramatic and emphatic use of parenthesis?
    A. The statue, after the museum paid five million dollars for it, turned out to be a fake.
    B. The statue—after the museum paid five million dollars for it—turned out to be a fake.
    C. The statue (after the museum paid five million dollars for it) turned out to be a fake.

Chapter 11
Restatement I

A writer must be careful to choose the right
words, rejecting some and welcoming others, and
place them so skillfully that even the common
ones seem fresh.
—Horace, *The Art of Poetry*

The term chosen for this and the following two chapters is *restatement* rather than
repetition in order to avoid the negative connotations surrounding the latter term. Certainly, repetition can be a vice when used thoughtlessly and ineffectively. On the other
hand, the strategic restatement of words and phrases enables the writer to stress an idea,
maintain or regain focus, define a term, and even enhance the stylistic quality of the
prose. This chapter presents the first of several devices useful for restatement.

11.1 Anaphora.

Anaphora (uh NAF or uh) involves the repetition of the same word or words at the
beginning of successive phrases, clauses, or sentences, often using climax (see Chapter 2,
Section 2.1) and parallelism (see Chapter 1, Section 1.1). The structure of anaphora can
be shown in a diagram, where the boxes represent the repeated words, and the dashes
represent the other, nonrepeated words: □—— □—— □——.

Often, the word or phrase repeated embodies a concept that the writer desires to
emphasize. In the following example, the idea of ignorance or lack of knowledge is
stressed.

> **Example 11.1.1**
> Slowly and grimly they advanced, not knowing what lay ahead, not knowing what they would find at the top of the hill, not knowing that they were so
> near to the outpost.

In the example below, Richard de Bury repeats the word *books* to maintain focus on
the concept of books themselves as he discusses the value of their variety.

> **Example 11.1.2**
> In books I find the dead as if they were alive; in books I foresee things to
> come; in books warlike affairs are set forth; from books come forth the laws of
> peace. —Richard de Bury

Note in the following example how Joshua Reynolds strengthens the idea of presenting an alternative view by repeating the phrase *instead of*.

Example 11.1.3

The wish of the genuine painter must be more extensive: Instead of endeavoring to amuse mankind with the minute neatness of his imitations, he must endeavor to improve them by the grandeur of his ideas; instead of seeking praise, by deceiving the superficial sense of the spectator, he must strive for fame by captivating the imagination. —Sir Joshua Reynolds

Anaphora is highly flexible and can be used with many kinds of construction. An often powerful use is to combine it with climax or with a focusing in or widening out to give a sense of context. Note in the following example how the concept moves from general to specific, while the repetition of the same word maintains thematic commonality.

Example 11.1.4

This has been a difficult time for the economy, a difficult time for the retail industry, and a difficult time for our clothing stores.

Anaphora can be used with questions that begin with the same word (such as *will, did, who, what, when, where, how, why*).

Example 11.1.5

Even after this victory, several issues remain unresolved. Will the policy be implemented? Will the implementation work? Will there be a continued rather than a momentary commitment to preserve it?

It can be used with negatives (*not, neither, nor, never, no, none, without*) to emphasize lack or denial.

Example 11.1.6

These lots are cheap, but they lack the infrastructure of habitation. There is no water, no electricity, no gas, no sewer, no telephone, no mail delivery.

Anaphora can be used with subordinating conjunctions (see Chapter 10, Style Check 10) to emphasize reasons (such as *because*), conditions (such as *if*) or other logical dependencies.

Example 11.1.7

If we can find fresh flashlight batteries, if we can get permission to leave the main cave, and if we can locate the formation, I will show you the stalagmite with the bat skeleton in it.

In most of the examples above, it is evident that anaphora creates something of a hammering effect, punching away at an idea, a qualification, a deficit, or some other meaning by repeating a word over and over. Thus, anaphora can be an aggressive device, especially if the repeated term is an aggressive one.

Example 11.1.8

Many Internet technology companies failed because they overspent on fancy offices and furniture, overspent on staffing, overspent on advertising, and overspent on hardware and software—all in the expectation of revenue that never quite appeared.

Exercise 11.1.1

Rewrite the following sentences, repeating the underlined word to create anaphora.
   (a) Their need to feel trendy resulted in a house filled with <u>designer</u> furniture, curtains, clothes, and even soap.
   (b) <u>We will search</u> in the hills, among the rocks, in the underbrush, over the whole area. And we will find the lost child.

11.2 Epistrophe.

Epistrophe (ē PIS trō fē) forms the counterpart to anaphora: The repetition of words or phrases comes at the end of successive phrases, clauses, or sentences, rather than at the beginning. The structure of epistrophe can be shown here in a diagram, where the boxes represent the repeated words, and the dashes represent the other, nonrepeated words: ——□   ——□   ——□.

In modern prose, the repetition is usually limited to two or three iterations, with four being used rarely for a particularly dramatic effect.

Example 11.2.1

In order for us to gain an understanding of the situation, the photographs and the electronic intercepts must be carefully analyzed, and the reports of operatives on the ground must be carefully analyzed.

Example 11.2.2

These cars are taking market share because their engineering is superior, the quality of their materials is superior, and the workmanship of their assembly is superior.

Example 11.2.3

That restaurant has many popular dishes, but it specializes in fried chicken and gravy, potatoes and gravy, biscuits and gravy, and gravy.

Note in the following example that epistrophe can be combined with climax (See Chapter 2, Section 2.1) and metanoia (see Chapter 5, Section 5.4) to create a highly dramatic effect.

Example 11.2.4

Her father did not permit his children to discuss imaginary worlds. He was a strict pragmatist, or rather a ruthless pragmatist, or perhaps even a vicious pragmatist.

Because the end of a word group (phrase, clause, or sentence) gains a natural stress, epistrophe creates a substantial degree of emphasis, as the examples above reveal. It is therefore useful for pointing up several aspects of an idea more demonstrably that would be the case without the repetition. Compare the emphases of the sentences in the examples below.

Example 11.2.5

Without epistrophe: The board of directors, while pretending to pursue stockholders' interests, is in fact engaged in the pursuit, consolidation, enjoyment, and abuse of power.

With epistrophe: The board of directors, while pretending to pursue stockholders' interests, is in fact engaged in the pursuit of power, the consolidation of power, the enjoyment of power, and the abuse of power.

Example 11.2.6

Without epistrophe: The student union presents a welcome feel: The carpet, the chairs, and the lighting are all soft.

With epistrophe: The student union presents a welcome feel: The carpet is soft, the chairs are soft, and the lighting is soft.

If you have a concept you wish to stress heavily, then epistrophe is often a good choice. Be careful to test your resulting sentence against the style of the remainder of your text, so that this usage does not stand out awkwardly as obviously rhetorical. (This advice holds for all the devices of repetition.) The more repetitions and the more words in the repeated material, the more intrusively rhetorical the sentence will appear. If, then, you wish to tone down the rhetoric, try reducing the number of repetitions or their length. Placing the repeated words farther apart also reduces the rhetorical feel, while maintaining the effect.

Example 11.2.7

What's wrong with eating so much processed food? Much of it contains an excessive amount of sugar. Look at the nutrition label and you will see that often the second or third ingredient—and remember that ingredients are listed in order of weight in the product—is sugar. Many products separately list fructose, sucrose, glucose, dextrose, and corn syrup, all basically types of sugar.

Exercise 11.2.1

Rewrite the following sentences, repeating the underlined word to create epistrophe.
(a) When the boy arrived home from school, his shoes, clothes, and books <u>were wet</u>.
(b) The international construction project required workers and financing <u>from many countries</u>.

11.3 Symploce.

Symploce (SIM plō kē) combines anaphora and epistrophe by repeating words at both the beginning and the ending of phrases, clauses, or sentences. The structure of symploce can be shown in a diagram, where the boxes represent some repeated words, the circles represent other repeated words, and the dashes represent the nonrepeated words: □——○ □——○.

Example 11.3.1

Whenever Chef Robaire cooked, his soup du jour began with chicken broth and garlic, his soup à la Chef included vegetables and garlic, and his soup Florentine was made with onions, cheese, and garlic.

Example 11.3.2

Without symploce: The probe can be used to read the exhaust gas temperature, and it makes a good temperature tester for ambient air.

With symploce: The probe can be used to read the exhaust gas temperature, and the probe makes a good tester for ambient air temperature.

One use of symploce is to set up a contrast or antithesis (see Chapter 1, Section 1.3). Note in the following example how the words *installed* and *maintained* are contrasted.

Example 11.3.3

It is not enough that smoke detectors be installed in every bedroom; smoke detectors must be maintained in every bedroom.

When the beginning and the end of relative short word groups remain the same, the difference in the middle is automatically highlighted.

Example 11.3.4
The electrical grid must guard against computer hackers—the grid is kept running by software, and the grid can be brought down by software.

Example 11.3.5
In her grief, she thought his death had destroyed her purpose; but through her grief, she used his death to strengthen her purpose.

Exercise 11.3.1
Rewrite the following sentences, repeating the underlined words to create symploce.
(a) The bill is generated and can be paid electronically.
(b) Place the outline at the beginning and the recap at the end of each chapter.

The following table summarizes the memory diagrams for the three devices in this chapter. The squares and circles represent repeated words, and the dashed lines represent the remaining text.

Diagrams for Schemes of Restatement I	
anaphora	□—— □—— □——
epistrophe	——□ ——□ ——□
symploce	□——O □——O

Style Check 11: Demetrius on Short Sentences for Emphasis.

Demetrius points out that short sentences are highly emphatic, even forceful, because they can express weighty matters in a few words. Note the difference:

Style Check Example 11.1
Not forceful: One of the fundamental tenets of the philosophy of ancient Greece was the idea that everyone should look inside himself or herself and seek self-knowledge.
Forceful: A cornerstone of Greek philosophy was, "Know thyself."

A short sentence puts the positions of emphasis (beginning and end) close together, thereby emphasizing the entire sentence. Short sentences are also easier to comprehend quickly.

Style Check Example 11.2

Not forceful: When you set sail, remember that there are many dangers in the ocean and that you have limited resources on board a relatively small watercraft, which will increase your risk substantially.

Forceful: When you set sail, remember that the sea is large and your boat is small.

The question might arise, If short sentences are easy to understand and emphatic, should all sentences be short? The answer is, No. Too many short sentences create a choppy and disjointed effect, causing writing to lose rhythm, movement, transition, and exactness (longer sentences are often needed in order to include qualification, detail, and context). Moreover, because short sentences are emphatic, readers will quickly tire from what seems to be an emphasis on everything. The result will be that where everything is emphasized, nothing is emphasized.

The most effective use of short sentences is to place them occasionally among—and especially after—longer sentences.

Style Check Example 11.3

Just as the engineering for this dam was a challenge, so the construction will be difficult and costly, involving blasting and moving more rock than the consortium has ever handled. But it can be done.

Note in the example above how effective the short sentence becomes by following a much longer one. The effect is almost like stretching and snapping a rubber band: The reader's attention is pulled out by the lengthy first sentence and then snapped back to focus on a short, quick comment that counterbalances the longer sentence.

Review Questions.

1. Match the rhetorical device with the appropriate example.

_____ A pseudo-event is deliberately staged and performed as news. In other words, a pseudo-event is imitation news.

_____ Our impatience makes us demand remedies that can be swallowed: pills to put us to sleep, pills to wake us, pills to makes us happy, pills for every ailment.

_____ The couple had obviously fallen in love with beige: The carpet was beige, the furniture was beige, and the walls were beige.

A. anaphora (but not symploce)

B. epistrophe (but not symploce)

C. symploce

2. The most effective use of a short sentence for emphasis is
    A. several short sentences together.
    B. a short sentence after one or more longer sentences.
    C. a short sentence before a longer sentence.

3. Anaphora, epistrophe, and symploce all create emphasis on the repeated terms or phrases because these devices
    A. exploit the natural emphasis given to the beginning and end of word groups.
    B. always include a strong contrast.
    C. stress words that would otherwise be easy to forget.

4. Match the example with the term.
    _____ epistrophe
    _____ symploce
    _____ anaphora
    A. above the runway, above the hills, above the clouds
    B. over the water, into the water, under the water
    C. quietly sitting in the chair, quietly nodding in the chair, quietly sleeping in the chair

5. Without looking at the Diagrams for Schemes of Restatement I on page 108, match the diagram to the name of the device.
    _____ ——☐ ——☐ ——☐
    _____ ☐—— ☐—— ☐——
    _____ ☐——○ ☐——○
    A. anaphora
    B. epistrophe
    C. symploce

Chapter 12
Restatement II

I have written quite a lot, but what I thought was
defective I have handed to the flames to revise.
—Ovid, *Tristia*

This chapter presents several additional methods of applying restatement effectively. As you study the examples, note how the repetition of the right word supplies connection, continuity, transition, and focus, as well as a smoothness of flow to the ideas.

12.1 Anadiplosis.

Anadiplosis (an uh di PLŌ sis) is formed by the repetition of the last word or words of a sentence or clause at or very near the beginning of the next. The immediate repetition calls attention to the words, reinforcing them. Remember, too, that the end and beginning of sentences are positions of emphasis. The structure of anadiplosis can be shown in a diagram, where the boxes represent the repeated words, and the dashes represent the other, nonrepeated words: ——☐ ☐——.

Example 12.1.1
The treatment plant has a record of uncommon reliability, a reliability envied by every other water treatment facility on the coast.

Example 12.1.2
Before investing in an opportunity that seems too good to be true, you should stop to think. Think about the likelihood of losing all your money.

Anadiplosis is useful for making clear the main point of the sentence by repeating the word or phrase that embodies that point.

Example 12.1.3
Early each morning, the quilter lit a three-hour candle and then began sewing, sewing on the quilt until the candle guttered.

Several repetitions can create both an elegant feel and a sense of logical progression to the ideas.

111

Example 12.1.4

In the library students can find books; in books they can find ideas; with ideas they can direct their lives to great achievements.

Example 12.1.5

After feeding, the lawn is watered. The water dissolves the fertilizer, and the fertilizer produces faster, healthier growth.

Exercise 12.1.1

Rewrite the following sentences, repeating the underlined word instead of using the pronoun, to create anadiplosis.

(a) Next weekend we will drive to Lava Beds National Monument to explore the <u>caves</u>. They are actually very interesting old lava tubes.

(b) The vast quantities of mineral nodules on the ocean floor are only one reminder of the value of <u>sea mining</u>; it is an opportunity yet unexploited in the quest for industrial metals.

12.2 Conduplicatio.

Conduplicatio (con doo plih KAHT ē ō) repeats a key word from a preceding clause or sentence at or near the beginning of the next. (Anadiplosis repeats the last word, but conduplicatio repeats a key word or words of the key idea to be continued in the next sentence, regardless of the position in the previous sentence.) The structure of conduplicatio can be shown in a diagram, where the boxes represent the repeated words, and the dashes represent the other, nonrepeated words: —□—— □——.

Example 12.2.1

Working adults form the largest single group of customers for on-line courses in the United States. On-line courses allow them to schedule academic assignments around full-time jobs and family responsibilities.

In the example above, notice that in the second sentence, the writer could have chosen to discuss working adults, customers, or on-line courses. Beginning the sentence with on-line courses immediately makes clear the continuing subject.

Example 12.2.2

Among the costs affecting the final price of foreign manufactured goods (including labor, materials, and shipping), import tariffs are perhaps the most commonly overlooked. Import tariffs can exceed 50 percent on some items, increasing their final cost dramatically.

Using conduplicatio provides a clear transition of thought from one sentence to another because it pulls out the important idea from the previous sentence and places it clearly at the front of the subsequent sentence, easily maintaining the reader's continuity of thought. When a sentence has several ideas in it, any one of which might be the subject of subsequent discussion, the use of conduplicatio instantly prevents any ambiguity. In the following example, notice that the first sentence contains several ideas, any one of which could be the subject of continued discussion: bestseller lists, voluntary reports, local bookstores, actual sales, nationwide sales.

Example 12.2.3

Bestseller lists are usually based on the voluntary reports of a few local bookstores and may not therefore reflect actual sales either regionally or nationwide. Voluntary reports are subject to the needs of the bookstore, which may wish to move a quantity of unsold inventory by naming it as a bestseller.

Notice that the writer began the second sentence with *voluntary reports*, in order to continue the paragraph by discussing the idea of the subjectivity of voluntary reports. Note that, depending on what idea the writer wished to continue, the second sentence could have begun in any of several ways, each using conduplicatio to provide a clear transition for the reader.

Example 12.2.3 continued

Sample alternative subsequent sentences in place of "Voluntary reports. . . ."

Local bookstore reports might not include sales by wholesale warehouses such as Costco or Sam's Club, and these outlets are known to move large quantities of some titles.

Bestseller lists should therefore be thought of more as marketing tools than as objective indicators of which titles are selling the most copies.

Nationwide sales may be substantially different from those tabulated for a particular locality.

This use of conduplicatio to pull out the idea intended for continued discussion is most valuable at the beginning of a paragraph, where the first sentence is often a topic sentence. When the reader has entered the paragraph only one sentence deep, the subject of focus may not yet be fully clear, especially when the first sentence includes several nouns and therefore provides several possible avenues of development. By pulling the idea to be developed out of the first sentence and, in the same word or words, putting it at the front of the next sentence, you quickly put your reader at ease by dispelling the uncertainty.

Exercise 12.2.1

Rewrite the following sentences, replacing the pronoun in the second sentence by repeating the underlined key word from the first sentence, to create conduplicatio. Rearrange the second sentence as necessary to put the repeated word at the beginning of the sentence.

    (a) Margarita fed the <u>goldfish</u> every day with the new pellets brought from Japan. After a few weeks, they began to turn a brighter orange.

    (b) Cleaning the years of yellowing varnish from the painting revealed that the men were sword fighting in the <u>daytime</u>, not at night. Why the men were squinting was now explained.

12.3 Epanalepsis.

Epanalepsis (ep an uh LEP sis) repeats the beginning word or words of a clause or sentence at the end. The structure of epanalepsis can be shown in a diagram, where the boxes represent the repeated words, and the dashes represent the other, nonrepeated words: □——□.

Placing the same idea in the two major positions of emphasis in the sentence calls attention to it, while the echo of the beginning at the end creates a feeling of return to the first thought, in spite of the intervening words.

Example 12.3.1

Water alone dug this giant canyon; yes, just ordinary water.

Example 12.3.2

To report that your committee is still investigating the incident is to tell us that you have nothing to report.

Many writers use epanalepsis to grant a truth or agree on common ground, and then show that the truth includes a deeper context.

Example 12.3.3

The theory sounds all wrong; but if the machine works, we cannot worry about theory.

Example 12.3.4

Our eyes saw it, but we could not believe our eyes.

The number of words intervening before the repetition may be many or few, as the following examples demonstrate.

Example 12.3.5

Enough these days never seems to be enough.

Example 12.3.6

A desert tortoise was crawling slowly along the road as I drove to work that morning; and on my way home I saw, a little farther down the road, the same desert tortoise.

Exercise 12.3.1

Rewrite the following sentences to create epanalepsis by repeating the underlined key word at the beginning and the end of the sentence.

(a) They may threaten <u>invasion</u>, but we will resist it.

(b) You may have wanted real <u>gold</u>, but it's only fool's gold you bought.

The following table summarizes the memory diagrams for the three devices in this chapter, together with the devices from Chapter 11. The squares and circles represent repeated words, and the dashed lines represent the remaining text.

Diagrams for Schemes of Restatement I & II	
anaphora	□—— □—— □——
epistrophe	——□ ——□ ——□
symploce	□——○ □——○
anadiplosis	——□ □——
conduplicatio	—□—— □——
epanalepsis	□——□

Style Check 12: Style.

Style refers to the form or verbal clothing of writing, the *way something is said*, as opposed to *what is said*, which is the subject matter itself. Meaning is a product of the combination of form and subject matter. Another way of thinking about this relationship is to say that form or style is a significant part of content.

Writing style influences the effect the content has on readers, how seriously readers take both the writer and the ideas expressed. For example, if the writer uses a flippant, breezy style, readers may view the content as less serious or less important than if the writer uses a more formal style. An overly formal style, on the other hand, may be less engaging for readers and make the writing more difficult to read through profitably.

Style is largely a product of each writer's linguistic habits: the words, phrases, and even sentence structures that have been adopted as the writer learned to read and write. However, there are several components of style that can be deliberately chosen in order to produce the quality of prose the writer desires.

- ◆ Proficiency. The grammatical and mechanical accuracy of writing sends a message to a reader about how knowledgeable, well educated, and competent a writer is. Competence also includes the appropriate coherence and flow of thought, focus on the ideas being discussed, and clarity of expression.
- ◆ Sentence structure. Whether sentences are long and complex or short and simple affects the way the ideas are received.
- ◆ Diction. The range of vocabulary, the level of abstractness, the precision of use, the presence or absence of clichés—all these affect the reader's perception of the writing.
- ◆ Components. The devices presented in this book are all stylistic options that, used carefully, can add beauty as well as clarity, emphasis, and personality to your writing.

In the table below are some terms often used to describe various writing styles. Which ones are appealing to you for your own style, and what will help you achieve that style?

Words Used to Describe Various Writing Styles			
affected	dense	luminous	rich
boring	engaging	opaque	sophisticated
bright	formal	open	stilted
clear	informal	ornate	stuffy
cold	interesting	pedantic	turgid
concise	lucid	plain	vague

Review Questions.

1. Match the rhetorical device with the appropriate example.

_____ When the investigators arrived, broken pottery was everywhere, and the kiln and turning wheel were also broken.

_____ The lightning bolt had traveled underground, melting the sand into a glassy rod. The glassy rod showed the path of the electricity from the bottom of the pole to the underground cable.

_____ The marriage counselor advised the couple to avoid the words *always* and *never* when discussing each other's behavior. Those words, he explained, could be especially hurtful.

A. anadiplosis

B. conduplicatio

C. epanalepsis

2. The joke, "He had nothing to say, but he surely said it well," reminds us that there is a distinction between
   A. meaning and intention.
   B. the how and the what of communication (form and content).
   C. rhetoric and seriousness.

3. Of the three devices discussed in this chapter, the one most useful for maintaining focus from one sentence to the next is
   A. anadiplosis.
   B. conduplicatio.
   C. epanalepsis.

4. Match the example with the term.
   _____ anadiplosis
   _____ conduplicatio
   _____ epanalepsis
   A. to be or not to be
   B. Jane wrote that she wanted to avoid "waistful" eating habits because habits are hard to break.
   C. In his hotel room, the spy saw a lizard, a bug, and a snake. The bug, however, was electronic.

5. Without looking at the Diagrams for Schemes of Restatement I & II on page 115, match the diagram to the name of the device.
   _____ —□—— □——
   _____ □——□
   _____ ——□ □——
   A. anadiplosis
   B. conduplicatio
   C. epanalepsis

Notes

Chapter 13
Restatement III

Rhetorical figures give power to our words, whether our goal is to strengthen the appeal of the argument, increase interest by adding variety to our expression, or communicate our ideas in the most proper and careful way.
—Quintilian, *Institutio Oratoria*

In this chapter are several final devices of restatement, providing you with some additional choices for developing strength, interest, clarity, and style in your writing. Use one of these devices when it will promote effective communication with your readers, not when it will call attention to itself and break your readers' concentration. Practice these devices as you develop your own style.

13.1 Diacope.

Diacope (dī AK uh pē) is the repetition of a word or phrase after an intervening word or phrase. In some uses, diacope might be thought of as a reshaped epanalepsis (see Chapter 12, Section 12.3), where the repeated beginning and ending are stretched out and the middle is condensed.

Example 13.1.1
They dynamited the statue, those villains; they dynamited the statue.

When the intervening words form a sentence or long string, parenthesis (see Chapter 10, Section 10.4) can be used to construct the interruption.

Example 13.1.2
The stock market didn't fall—will you believe it?—the stock market didn't fall.

In the examples above, the repetition occurs at the beginning and ending of the sentences. However, the repetition can occur anywhere in the sentence. Note in the following two examples that the repeated words can be at the beginning (Example 13.1.3) or at the end (Example 13.1.4).

Example 13.1.3

The motto on the building—and I quote it—the motto on the building says, "Equal justice under law."

Example 13.1.4

Clandestine intervention into that government's affairs has been attempted before, and the result was a disaster. Yes, that's the word, a disaster.

Often, the intervening expression is an expletive (see Chapter 2, Section 2.4) or other interrupting word.

Example 13.1.5

The project was three months late, of course, three months late.

Example 13.1.6

Words become copyrighted the moment they are written down, to be sure, the moment they are written down.

Diacope's main use, as these examples demonstrate, is for emphasis, or to restart a thought after a parenthetical interruption. In many uses, this device includes a rhetorical edge to it that reminds the reader of a speech (where it has been popularly used for centuries). Be careful, then, that the effect you produce is a desired effect.

Exercise 13.1.1

Rewrite the following sentences, creating diacope by repeating the underlined words and adding a few appropriate words as an intervening expression.

(a) The bite of a leech is <u>completely painless</u> because the leech produces an anesthetic that numbs the area it bites.

(b) <u>Toll road charges now increase</u> during busier times of the day.

13.2 Epizeuxis.

Epizeuxis (ep i ZOOK sis) is the repetition of one word or short phrase. The most common and most natural effect is produced by three occurrences of the word or phrase, while two can be effective as well.

Example 13.2.1

The best way to describe this portion of South America is lush, lush, lush.

Compare the uses in the following example.

Example 13.2.2

Without epizeuxis: When you attempt to frame this scene in the viewfinder of the camera, what you see is not trees and mountains, but wires.

With epizeuxis: When you attempt to frame this scene in the viewfinder of the camera, what you see is not trees and mountains, but wires, wires, and more wires.

A primary use and effect of epizeuxis is to present the idea that there is a large amount of whatever is being repeated—that repetition is required, not merely for emphasis, but to cover the quantity being described, as if a single word could not perform the task by itself. The examples above demonstrate this use. On the other hand, the word repeated can refer to something other than a large quantity, as the examples below reveal. In these cases, emphasis is the primary effect.

Example 13.2.3

The couple returned to the mobile home park where their home had been the day before the tornado. They looked at the rubble and shook their heads. Their home was all gone, all gone.

Example 13.2.4

To complete the process of mounting the computer chip, a robotic spot welder connected the tiny, tiny wires from the chip to the carrier that plugged into the motherboard.

Example 13.2.5

As they walked back to the car, the beachgoers suddenly realized that the sand was hot, hot, hot.

The most common position for the epizeuxis repetition is at the end of the sentence, but you should not feel limited to this. As example 13.2.4 shows, the repetition (*tiny, tiny*) can be in the middle. The beginning of the sentence is another useful position.

Example 13.2.6

Without epizeuxis: "Free!" is all I hear from the advertisers these days. And yet they want me to spend.

With epizeuxis: "Free! free! free!" is all I hear from the advertisers these days. And yet they want me to spend, spend, spend.

Example 13.2.7

The distant, distant hills seemed to call out to them as they sat on the hot rocks of the hot valley, saying quietly, "Come to me; come to me."

Exercise 13.2.1

Rewrite the following sentences to create epizeuxis.

    (a) The faded watercolor painting was still valuable because of its pale beauty.

    (b) The speaker realized his need for improvement when he looked up from his notes and saw yawns.

13.3 Antimetabole.

Antimetabole (an tē muh TAB uh lē) reverses the order of repeated words or phrases to call attention to the final formulation, present alternatives, or show contrast. The structure is loosely chiastic (see Chapter 1, Section 1.2), using an AB-BA form.

Example 13.3.1

All play and no work can be as stressful as all work and no play.

Example 13.3.2

Sarah's job is to find a location suitable for the wedding, while Alison's job is to design a wedding suitable for the location.

A frequent use of antimetabole is to present a correction of an idea or attitude.

Example 13.3.3

Ask not what your country can do for you, but what you can do for your country. —John F. Kennedy

Example 13.3.4

Instead of seeking more publicity in order to increase sales, we should seek more sales in order to increase publicity.

Example 13.3.5

The question we ask in gerontology is not, "How can a senior citizen take care of a pet?" but, "How can a pet take care of a senior citizen?"

The reversal can involve only a few words, as the underlined words demonstrate in the example below.

Example 13.3.6

In the future, we will rent everything and own nothing: We will no longer <u>continue to pay</u> on a mortgage but will <u>pay to continue</u> a rental.

Antimetabole is overtly rhetorical and calls attention to itself. Its use and placement, therefore, need to be strategically considered. The end of a section or paragraph concluding a point or an argument often provides a good opportunity for an antimetabole, where the reversal of thought, combined with the rhetorical effect, makes clear that a thought is being concluded, and concluded vigorously.

Exercise 13.3.1

Rewrite the following sentences, completing each one by reversing the underlined words, to create antimetabole.

    (a) There was mutual benefit: <u>The company helped Jones</u> and. . . .

    (b) Some advertisements are as memorable as the product: <u>The ad reminds us of the product</u> and. . . .

13.4 Scesis Onomaton.

Scesis Onomaton (SKĒ sis uh NŌ muh tahn) emphasizes an idea by expressing it in a string of generally synonymous phrases or statements. The repetition garners attention for an idea by dwelling on it, and at the same time the various restatements allow the writer to present a richer view of the idea through multiple ways of expressing it.

Example 13.4.1

Wendy lay there, motionless in a peaceful slumber, very still in the arms of sleep.

Example 13.4.2

The fog rolled in so thick that we had no visibility; we were completely blinded; we just could not see anything.

Example 13.4.3

Warning! Misuse of this product could result in great bodily injury. You could be harmed severely.

The obvious use of redundancy sometimes produces a slightly humorous effect when the reader realizes that the same idea is being conveyed repeatedly.

Example 13.4.4

There is one thing the park proponents overlook: Such a plan would be extremely costly, horrendously expensive, and require truckloads of money.

Example 13.4.5

We reached the goal, we met the target, we hit the numbers, we made our objective!

Note from the examples above that as the seriousness of the context increases, the number of effective repetitions becomes fewer. A good starting point for your thinking is to consider two synonymous expressions for highly serious or sensitive material (as in Example 13.4.3) and three for most other purposes that are not intended to be deliberately humorous.

Exercise 13.4.1

Rewrite the following sentences, adding one or two synonymous expressions to the underlined expression, to create a scesis onomaton. Feel free to consult a thesaurus for help with synonyms, if needed. However, avoid uncommon or difficult words.

(a) The cloth felt <u>smooth and soft</u>.
(b) The mountain climbers <u>carried the heavy supplies</u> themselves.

Style Check 13: Demetrius on Increasing Vividness.

For maximum effectiveness, Demetrius recommends that words be arranged in the order of increasing vividness and strength, so that greater and more forceful images and ideas replace lesser ones. The result is that the ideas build and brighten as their visual power grows.

Style Check Example 13.1

John Milton's best work, his distinguished masterpiece, is *Paradise Lost*.

Here, *distinguished masterpiece* is more forceful than the more ordinary *best work*.

Style Check Example 13.2

The pot lay there broken, its shattered and disfigured pieces lying in a brown heap.

Here, the visual quality of the sentence increases from the less descriptive *broken* to the more exact and even colorful *shattered, disfigured pieces*, and *brown heap*.

Compare the difference between these two sentences:

Style Check Example 13.3

The sunlight entered at the high window and flooded across the desk.
The sunlight flooded across the desk after it entered at the high window.

In this example, the sense of flooding is vivid, while the word *entered* is neutral. The first sentence is strong because the vividness increases. The second sentence is weak because the idea drops from flooding to merely entering.

Visual characteristics are critical to good writing because pictures aid your reader greatly. The reader's ability to follow your thinking and to understand your ideas is increased when you provide images. (Concrete writing—writing that uses image-producing words—is more easily processed than highly abstract writing.) By arranging your words in the order of increasing vividness, you create the effect of increasing clarity, of growing understanding on the part of your reader. Such an effect not only aids comprehension but helps to maintain interest.

Review Questions.

1. Match the rhetorical device with the appropriate example.
   _____ That night the water came down, the rain fell, the drops descended.
   _____ Tonight's homework? I have to read, read, read, read.
   _____ The window tinting film will fail first around the edges—if anywhere at all—first around the edges.
   _____ Today, instead of looking for an amusement area that contains a restaurant, people look for a restaurant that contains an amusement area.
   A. diacope
   B. epizeuxis
   C. antimetabole
   D. scesis onomaton

2. Which example represents increasing vividness the best?
   A. The rotisserie chickens cooked slowly, the hot coals slowly making them tender.
   B. The rotisserie chickens cooked slowly over the hot coals, which glowed orange and white amid the black and gray ashes, spitting and sparking as the juices dripped from above.
   C. The rotisserie chickens cooked slowly over the hot coals, which seemed to grow hotter as they burned and roasted the birds more and more completely, making them tender and delicious.

3. Of the four devices of repetition discussed in this chapter, which one would be most useful for providing a fuller and more detailed picture of the repeated idea?
   A. diacope
   B. epizeuxis
   C. antimetabole
   D. scesis onomaton

4. Match the example with the term.

_____ diacope

_____ epizeuxis

_____ antimetabole

_____ scesis onomaton

A. Aristotle noted that not only do our beliefs shape our actions but also that our actions shape our beliefs.

B. All of the walls are stonework: rocks piled up, stones cemented together, slabs fitted to each other.

C. Time is passing, I tell you, time is passing. We must act quickly.

D. The three most important factors in retailing are location, location, location.

5. Match the clue with the term.

_____ words, of course, words

_____ A should not verb B, but B should verb A

_____ word, word, word

_____ synonym, synonym, synonym

A. diacope

B. epizeuxis

C. antimetabole

D. scesis onomaton

Chapter 14
Sound

Beautiful words contribute to an elegant style.
—Demetrius, *On Style*

As mentioned in Style Check 1 at the end of the first chapter, most readers subvocalize when they read silently, thus making the rhythm of your writing an important aspect. In addition to rhythm, writing has sounds, sounds that readers hear in their minds as they read. The devices in this chapter will help you add pleasantness to the sound of your writing.

14.1 Alliteration.

Alliteration (uh lit uh RĀ shun) is formed by repeating the same sound at the beginning of successive words or words related to each other in some way. The most familiar form of alliteration is the repetition of consonants in word pairs.

> **Example 14.1.1**
> *Without alliteration:* The late delivery of parts resulted in an unwanted delay in production.
> *With alliteration:* The late delivery of parts resulted in a disheartening delay in production.

In the example above, *disheartening delay* is alliterated because both words in the phrase begin with the consonant sound *d*.

As the example below shows, alliterated phrases such as *mature marriage* are memorable because they call a little extra attention to themselves and because of the repetition of initial consonant sound.

> **Example 14.1.2**
> *Without alliteration:* Jonathan was the child of mature parents, who were calm and relaxed.
> *With alliteration:* Jonathan was the product of a mature marriage, whose partners were calm and relaxed.

Alliteration adds not only a bit of music to your writing but an emphasis on ideas that will help your reader recall a key concept better. Note the difference between *remembered regard* and *remembered esteem* in the following example.

Example 14.1.3

Without alliteration: After she grew up, she never forgot those words of praise. This treasure of remembered esteem stayed with her throughout her adult life.

With alliteration: After she grew up, she never forgot those words of praise. This treasure of remembered regard stayed with her throughout her adult life.

Consonant clusters, such as *st, cl, pl, fl, sp, gr*, etc., are also useful for alliterating.

Example 14.1.4

Without alliteration: Everywhere they looked they saw the crawling bugs of the insect world.

With alliteration: Everywhere they looked they saw the crawling creatures of the insect world.

In the example below, the alliterative phrase *problem of protein* contains an intervening word, *of.*

Example 14.1.5

The challenge of world hunger is the problem of protein: Finding a source of inexpensive protein is a major goal of our organization.

Many alliterations are constructed with unstressed syllables between the stressed, alliterated syllables, as in *filthy to filtered* and *stuck in a stack* in the examples below.

Example 14.1.6

Without alliteration: After the water passes through Stage 3, it has gone from dirty to filtered.

With alliteration: After the water passes through Stage 3, it has gone from filthy to filtered.

Example 14.1.7

Without alliteration: The letter remained stuck in a pile of forgotten papers.
With alliteration: The letter remained stuck in a stack of forgotten papers.

While it is common for alliterated words to be next to or close to each other, words widely separated can also be alliterated if they share some relationship that connects them. A typical relationship is that of antithesis (see Chapter 1, Section 1.3). Note the antithetical positions of *temerity* and *temperateness* in the example below.

Example 14.1.8

Without alliteration: Within a month, and to the surprise of his friends, he had transformed himself from an icon of rashness into a model of temperateness.

With alliteration: Within a month, and to the surprise of his friends, he had transformed himself from an icon of temerity into a model of temperateness.

Parallelism is another way to incorporate widely parted alliterated words. In the example below, *darkness* and *depressed* come at the end of loosely parallel phrases.

Example 14.1.9

The experiment studied the connection between lighting and mood. Specifically, it asked whether there might be a connection between the time spent in darkness and the likelihood of being depressed.

Alliteration is now understood to include the repetition of initial vowel sounds, also. Note the *o* sounds in *open, ovens,* and *overemphasized* in the next example and the *a* sound in *attacked, angry,* and *ants* in the subsequent example.

Example 14.1.10

Without alliteration: The danger of failing to close oven doors cannot be stressed enough.

With alliteration: The danger of open ovens cannot be overemphasized.

Example 14.1.11

Without alliteration: The hiker was quickly set upon by the enraged ants.

With alliteration: The hiker was soon attacked by the angry ants.

As the examples above demonstrate, alliteration often consists of more than two words. As in Examples 14.1.10 and 14.1.11, there may be two alliterating words together, followed by one or more intervening words before further alliteration. In other cases, several alliterating words can be placed together.

Example 14.1.12

Without alliteration: This ozone air cleaner uses a patented antipollution system for the cleanest air imaginable.

With alliteration: This ozone air cleaner uses a patented purification process for the cleanest air possible.

As always, the best test of this device is effectiveness. Alliteration can be created to suit any level of formality and audience; the challenge is to make a good match. Remember, too, that an excessive amount of alliteration becomes silly and produces an immature feeling to your writing, so be careful not to get carried away. For formal writing, an occasional alliterated word pair (such as *competitive components*) is often the best choice. The most attractive alliteration is the freshest. Be cautious about using existing alliterations that have become common or even trite, as in *purple prose, constant companion,* or *tricky trivia.*

Exercise 14.1.1

Write sentences containing alliteration according to each instruction.

(a) Write a promotional sentence for a resort on the ocean, with an alliterative phrase involving the waterfront (that is, alliterate *beach* or *coast* or *shore* or another, similar word).

(b) Write a sentence that alliteratively describes people who are alone during the holidays. Take care that the alliteration is serious and not flippant.

14.2 Onomatopoeia.

An onomatopoeia (on uh mat uh PĒ uh) is a word that, when pronounced, imitates the sound the word names. Another way of saying this is that the word imitates its meaning. For example, when spoken, the word *plop* is intended to resemble the sound of a small object splashing into water or another liquid. The resemblance between the word and the actual sound is often more conventional than actual, so that some degree of imagination must be used. For example, the word *slam* is a rather poor mimic of the actual sound made by closing a door swiftly, yet the pronunciation makes a closer imitation of the sound than the word *close*.

Onomatopoeias add not only interesting and lively sounds to writing, but they also often involve distinctive movements of the mouth to pronounce, thereby adding to their effect. In the following examples, compare the increased aural (sound) sensation contributed by the onomatopoeias, and note also how much your mouth moves to pronounce them. (Read the sentences aloud for the best effect.)

Example 14.2.1

Without onomatopoeia: Someone yelled, "Look out!" just as I heard the stopping of tires and the horrible noise of bending metal and breaking glass.

With onomatopoeia: Someone yelled, "Look out!" just as I heard the loud screeching of tires followed by a grinding, wrenching crash.

Example 14.2.2

Without onomatopoeia: The mosquitoes flying around their ears kept the botanists from completing their experiment in the swamp.

With onomatopoeia: The mosquitoes buzzing and whizzing around their ears kept the botanists from completing the experiment in the swamp.

Example 14.2.3

Without onomatopoeia: No one talks in these factories. Everyone is too busy. The only sounds are the scissors and the sewing machines, working continuously.

With onomatopoeia: No one talks in these factories. Everyone is too busy. The only sounds are the snip, snip of scissors and the droning hum of sewing machines.

Example 14.2.4

Without onomatopoeia: I loved that old car. The constant noise it made on a rough road and that special sound whenever I hit a bump are treasures I'll always remember.

With onomatopoeia: I loved that old clunker. The incessant rattle it made on a rough road and that squeakity-squeak whenever I hit a bump are treasures I'll always remember.

Some onomatopoeias produce a more satisfying sound effect than others, so be sure to choose well. Note the improvement in the following example:

Example 14.2.5

Original: If you like the dripping of a faucet at three o'clock in the morning, you will like this group's music.

Improved: If you like the plop, plop, plop of a faucet at three o'clock in the morning, you will like this group's music.

In the example above, *dripping* (an onomatopoeia) is improved upon both by substituting a more sonic word (*plop*) and by repeating it to generate the full effect of the dripping faucet. (See the discussion of epizeuxis in Chapter 13, Section 13.2, for more about repeating a word for effect.)

Onomatopoeias fall into two categories: the traditional ones (found in most dictionaries) and the nontraditional ones. In the traditional group are the conventionalized imitations of sounds such as *crack* and *wham*. (Note that while these words may not sound exactly like the sound they pretend to imitate, they do make a distinctive sound when pronounced.)

In the nontraditional group are those words that truly attempt to imitate a sound but have no conventionalized spelling. For example, cartoonist Don Martin suggests that the final sound a toilet makes at the end of its flush should be spelled *galook*. Other examples of nontraditional onomatopoeias are *bzzzt*, *flumph*, and *gack*.

On the next page is a table containing many traditional onomatopoeias, followed by a table containing some nontraditional ones. As a rule, you are safe using traditional onomatopoeias in all levels of writing, from formal to highly informal. The nontraditional ones are welcome in informal writing and may be used in formal writing if your subject, audience, and circumstances permit.

Examples of Traditional Onomatopoeic Words

babble	clack	howl	snap
bang	clang	hum	sniffle
bark	clap	jingle	splash
bash	clatter	meow	splat
bawl	click	moan	splatter
beep	cluck	mumble	spurt
belch	cockadoodledoo	munch	sputter
blab	crack	murmur	squeak
blam	crackle	neigh	squirt
blare	crash	oink	thud
bleat	creak	ouch	thump
blurt	crunch	plink	trickle
boing	cuckoo	plop	tromp
bong	ding	pop	tweet
bonk	drip	purr	whack
boo hoo	flutter	rattle	wham
boom	gasp	rip	wheeze
bop	gobble	screech	whir
bow wow	groan	sizzle	whoosh
bump	growl	slam	woof
burp	gurgle	slap	yahoo
buzz	gush	slash	zap
cheep	hack	slurp	zing
chirp	hiss	smack	zip
chomp	honk	smash	zoom

Examples of Nontraditional Onomatopoeic Words

arf	gack	pow	urp
brrr	galook	psssh	vroom
bzzt	grrr	psst	whump
doink	klunk	ribbit	whunk
flumph	ksssh	shhh	zot

Exercise 14.2.1

Rewrite each of the following sentences, substituting onomatopoeic words for the underlined, more general, descriptive words.

(a) The strange animal sounds we heard in the forest frightened us.

(b) The frying steak smelled wonderful.

14.3 Assonance.

Assonance (AS uh nuns) is created by repeating vowel sounds in the stressed syllables of successive words or words relatively close to each other. In either case, the vowels occur next to different ending consonants, as in *dote, soul, moan*. (If the vowels were next to the same ending consonants, rhyme would result: *dole, soul, mole*.)

Assonance creates a subtle but elegant effect. In the following example, note how the repetition of the short *i* in *city, hill,* and *hid* contributes to the rhythm and music of the sentence.

Example 14.3.1
A city that is set on a hill cannot be hid. —Matthew 5:14b (KJV)

In formal prose, while rhyming would be inappropriate, assonance allows the writer to include a feeling of rhythm and sound that is perfectly acceptable. In the example below, the repeated long *o* sounds in the underlined words create a drawn-out sonorousness, suggesting both flow and inevitability of movement.

Example 14.3.2
<u>So</u> <u>flows</u> the river, <u>going</u> past the town, its <u>whole</u> <u>load</u> of toxins, fish, and sediment <u>pouring</u> <u>evermore</u> into the sea.

In many cases, assonance is used for a pair of words next to each other.

Example 14.3.3
The aim of the portrait photographer is to <u>freeze</u> a <u>gleam</u> in the eye.

Example 14.3.4
Despite its lengthy and impressive provenance, the supposedly faded print was merely a <u>pale</u> <u>fake</u>.

As long as the assonance is effective, several words can be used, and they can be placed anywhere. The assonance must occur in stressed syllables, however.

Example 14.3.5
To get within <u>sight</u> of the lava, the geologists took a <u>high</u>-temperature <u>hike</u>.

Example 14.3.6
The <u>hoot</u> of the owl in the <u>cool</u> of the <u>moonlight</u> warned them to head home <u>soon</u>.

Remember—and the third reminder should be enough—many readers subvocalize as they read, so these sounds are not lost on them. The music—or noise—of your prose will be heard, at least at some level. The subtlety of effect of assonance means that your readers will probably not remark on its presence (the same is true for the use of many of the devices in this book). Rather, instead of thinking, "My, that's assonance," or "My, that's musical," they will think, "My, that's well written." Nevertheless, the sounds are there in an affecting way. Pay attention, then, to the sound of your writing. Read it aloud to get the feel of it and to test its aural qualities.

Exercise 14.3.1

Write a sentence containing assonance, according to each instruction, for a total of two sentences. <u>Underline the assonance</u>. Remember that assonance differs from alliteration (initial vowel sound) and rhyme (same ending sound). Feel free to use the example words if you want.

(a) Include at least two words, producing assonance with a long *a* sound. Example words are *stain, rate, ladle, make, paid, sake, tail, wave*.

(b) Include at least two words, producing assonance with a short *i* sound. Example words are *fit, hint, bill, dig, grin, list, nibble, pick, tip*.

14.4 Consonance.

Consonance (KON suh nuns) is formed by repeating the same consonant sound at the end of stressed syllables (or short words) with different vowels before the consonants. Note the repeated *p* sound at the end of *rip, cap,* and *top* in the example below.

Example 14.4.1

Without consonance: He was so thirsty that he tried to tear the lid from the top.
With consonance: He was so thirsty that he tried to rip the cap from the top.

As the example above shows, consonance might be thought of as backwards alliteration: Instead of initial consonant sounds, consonance is formed by ending consonant sounds. The vowels must differ; otherwise, rhyme rather than consonance would result.

Example 14.4.2

Consonance: Sitting on the sandbar, the <u>flat</u>-bottomed <u>boat</u> began to <u>rot</u>.
Rhyme: Sitting on the sandbar, the <u>boat</u> in the <u>moat</u> would not <u>float</u>.

As with assonance and alliteration, in formal writing, consonance is often restricted to two or three words in a sentence.

Example 14.4.3

The committee has tried repeatedly to <u>stall</u> this <u>bill</u>, but we will soon bring it to the floor for a vote.

The strictest form of consonance is constructed by matching the consonants before and after the different vowels, as in *flip* and *flop* or *tick* and *tock*. In fact, many paired-word expressions (some of which have now become single words) use this form of consonance, as the table below reveals.

Examples of Two-Word Consonance		
bing-bong	flip-flop	plip-plop
brick-a-brack	hip-hop	singsong
click-clack	King Kong	splish-splash
clip-clop	Kit-Kat®	Tic-Tac®
criss-cross	knick-knack	tick-tock
ding-dong	mishmash	tip-top
flim-flam	Ping-Pong®	tit-for-tat

Example 14.4.4

The man with the <u>lump</u> on his head tried to <u>limp</u> into the emergency room.

Example 14.4.5

The termite fumigation will kill every <u>pest</u> in every <u>post</u> in the house.

Exercise 14.4.1

Write a sentence containing consonance, according to each instruction, for a total of two sentences. <u>Underline the consonance.</u> Feel free to use the example words if you want.

    (a) Include at least two words, producing consonance with an ending *d* sound. Example words are *led, deed, rid, mode, ride, blood, food.*

    (b) Include at least two words, producing consonance with an ending *k* sound. Example words are *brick, luck, rock, make, fluke, poke, hack.*

As an aid to help you remember and distinguish among the devices in this chapter, here is the Duck Story.

    ◆ If it <u>walks</u> and <u>waddles</u> like a duck, it's alliteration.

    ◆ If it <u>quacks</u> like a duck, it's onomatopoeia.

    ◆ If it <u>flies</u> <u>like</u> a duck, it's assonance.

    ◆ If it <u>looks</u> <u>like</u> a duck, it's consonance.

Style Check 14: Texture.

Writing that maintains readers' attention is usually writing with texture: writing that makes sensory appeals. Whenever you sit down to consider a writing task, then, think of your subject and audience with the question of how to appeal to the senses. Here are a few ideas.

Sight. Use concrete words that produce images. Use metaphors, analogies, similes.

Sound. Use devices from this chapter. Use onomatopoeia, alliteration, assonance.

Smell. Use suggestive diction, including images related to aromatic things: *perfume, smoke.*

Touch. Use words that suggest touching: *touch, feel, handle, grasp, grip, caress, grab, finger.*

Taste. Use words that remind readers of food. Use words that require the mouth to work more than usual to pronounce them, especially with *s* or *sh* sounds: *crushed, rocks, machinery.* See if you can get your readers slurping.

No one has yet calculated how many million words per second are being written on this planet, but there are certainly too many for any writing to stand out if it has the personality of tepid, weak tea.

Review Questions.

1. Match the rhetorical device with the appropriate example.
     _____ Chomp into this new breadstick for that crunchy taste.
     _____ Our goal is to have the brightest float on the street.
     _____ The line from the kite snagged high in the tree.
     _____ The chef pulled the blue-bladed knife from the rack.
     A. alliteration
     B. onomatopoeia
     C. assonance
     D. consonance

2. Match the device with the question.
     _____ Which device employs vowel sounds in the middle of words?
     _____ Which device employs the repeated initial letters of words?
     _____ Which device employs words whose pronunciation imitates sounds?
     _____ Which device employs consonant sounds at the end of words?
     A. alliteration
     B. onomatopoeia
     C. assonance
     D. consonance

3. If you made up a new word to represent the sound of a spring flying out of a wind-up toy, you would be constructing a(n)
   A. alliteration.
   B. onomatopoeia.
   C. assonance.
   D. consonance.

4. The sounds associated with words are important even for silent readers because many readers
   A. read everything aloud.
   B. subvocalize as they read.
   C. remember being read to as children.

5. One way to think of the texture of writing is the degree to which it
   A. has a mix of long and short words.
   B. feels smooth on the tongue.
   C. appeals to the senses.

Notes

Chapter 15
Drama

Every style—formal, semi-formal, and familiar—is made more dignified through the use of rhetorical ornaments, when they are scattered widely to add color and texture to the discourse.
—Cicero, *Ad Herennium*

By creating a degree of dramatic effect, the devices in this chapter enable you to add a feeling of presence to your writing, a sense of real-time discussion, even a moderate amount of intensity. Because each of these devices implies either interaction with the reader or a work in progress (like the flow of speech), their use produces a sense of immediacy, as if your readers are witnessing the work being written.

15.1 Rhetorical Question.

A rhetorical question differs from hypophora (see Chapter 4, Section 4.3) in that the writer does not answer it because the answer is self-evident. In other words, the expected answer is implied by the question itself, and is often just a *yes* or *no*. In the example below, the expected answer is clearly, No, because businesses cannot function by losing ever-increasing amounts of money.

> **Example 15.1.1**
> So, then, do we want to continue a business model that guarantees we will lose more money next year than this year and more money than ever each coming year?

In the example below, the implied answer is, Yes.

> **Example 15.1.2**
> Shouldn't parents be encouraged to join with the school in the children's summer reading program? After all, parents and guardians will be the ones who must monitor and encourage their children's reading at home.

Of course, a reader could conceivably answer, No, but the *rhetorically desired* answer is clearly a Yes. If the writer did not want to imply an answer, a straightforward question rather than a rhetorical question would have been asked: "Should parents be encouraged. . . ."

Often, even though the answer is clearly implied, the rhetorical question will be the stimulus for further discussion.

Example 15.1.3

How can drainage and soil erosion be considered an individual homeowner issue when the water and soil flowing from one lot will pour out onto other lots in the development? What we need is an association-wide plan that involves a systematized drainage and erosion control, linking the drainage from backyards and downspouts to. . . .

Sometimes, the implied answer becomes clear by the context of the question, especially by the discussion leading up to it.

Example 15.1.4

The new tomatoes were genetically selected for traits that would facilitate mechanical harvesting: toughness of skin, evenness of ripening, hardiness of bush, high percentage of blossom-set to fruit. Taste to humans fell off the list. Is it any wonder, then, that the produce department's tomatoes of today lack the flavor of those of years past?

When carefully done, several rhetorical questions together can result in a well-developed paragraph.

Example 15.1.5

We fear risk, yet which of our actions is accompanied by no risk at all? We feel anxious before doing something for the first time, yet what habit do we have that was not once a first-time event? Could we ever make progress without risk? Would we ever gain a new friend without a first word of greeting?

Example 15.1.6

Given the number of thoughtful and intelligent people who have made fools of themselves trying to predict the future ("Airplane flight is impossible," "Television is a passing fad"), is it any wonder that most futurists are so cautious? Given the unpredictable interactions between and uses for new inventions, can anyone really say what the impact of a new product will be? And given the surprising and often unexpected history of technology over the past fifty years, can we even imagine with any accuracy what we might hold in our hands, sit in, or eat in the next fifty years?

Rhetorical question should be used to allow your readers to think and conclude along with you. If the question is absurd or manipulative, you will probably lose your readers' respect. Be especially careful when writing several questions together, as in Example 15.1.5, because too much leading becomes heavy-handed and offensive.

Exercise 15.1.1

Rewrite the following sentences, converting each from a statement into a rhetorical question.

Example sentence: It is not wise to allow federal dietary guidelines to be influenced by political pressure from food producers.

Example conversion: Is it wise to allow federal dietary guidelines to be influenced by political pressure from food producers?

(a) The gore film, with its lurid chemical blood and wiggly silicone guts, is not the best we can expect from the film industry.

(b) The senator should not be impeached for acting in error but in good faith.

15.2 Aporia.

Aporia (uh PŌR ē uh) expresses doubt about a fact, idea, or conclusion. The doubt may be real or pretended. An expression of uncertainty is useful for presenting alternatives without favoring one or the other, as in the following examples.

Example 15.2.1

I cannot decide whether I approve of dress codes for middle-school children: Dress codes prevent gang clothing and conspicuous consumption, but they also produce a gray uniformity that suppresses personality and individual taste.

Example 15.2.2

When I see youngsters playing kill-everyone video games at an arcade, I wonder: Is the simulated violence a healthy outlet for purging their aggressions or an unhealthy stimulus that reinforces them?

A noncommittal expression similar to the ones above can provide a conclusion to a discussion that you do not want to continue, or it can begin an examination of the alternatives in more detail. That is, an expression of doubt can be an excellent way to introduce a discussion that resolves or attempts to resolve the doubt. Expressing aporia as a two-way question, as in Example 15.2.2 above, provides a helpful structure for discussing the arguments on each side. (See the discussion of hypophora in Chapter 4, Section 4.3.)

Aporia can also be used to acknowledge and then pass over claims that you deem peripheral to your discussion or simply do not want to address directly. The expression of doubt about the claims allows you to notice them officially (to show you are aware of them and to position your own point in context) and then put them politely aside without either accepting or rejecting them.

Example 15.2.3

I do not know what effect the new shopping center might have on the downtown retailers, or whether overall prices for groceries and clothing will change, but I do believe that traffic on Route 71 will be increased substantially, and with the traffic, noise and accidents.

Example 15.2.4

Yes, I realize that the investment broker has an official assay report showing that the mine should yield twenty pounds of gold per ton of ore, and I am uncertain about what to say to that. What I do know is that the richest African mines yield only about three ounces of gold per ton of ore.

Here in Example 15.2.4, the writer has decided to plead ignorance about the meaning of the assay report and then to supply some significant comparative information, rather than to claim that the investment broker is obviously a confidence artist with a wildly unrealistic (and therefore probably phony) assay.

In a similar way, aporia can be used to cast doubt in a polite and understated way or to indicate the need for further deliberation.

Example 15.2.5

I am not so sure I can completely accept the CEO's rationale for buying a corporate jet to be used instead of the commercial airlines.

Example 15.2.6

I have not yet been fully convinced that the defendant's alibi is unimpeachable. Can we meet again to discuss this further?

Aporia is also effective for expressing doubt over the ranking of several things perceived to be of similar value (whether good or bad).

Example 15.2.7

I do not know who is worse: those who dump their toxic waste into our rivers and cause cancer or those who dilute the anticancer drugs that could fight it.

In the example above, note how aporia has been used to set up an analogy of sorts. Deliberating over the precedence between dumping carcinogenic waste and diluting anticancer drugs creates a comparison between the two actions, with the implication that they are ethically similar enough to warrant the comparison. (The comparison would be more clearly an analogy if the surrounding discussion were about the medicine.)

Instead of expressing the writer's uncertainty about a position, aporia can express uncertainty over what others may know. Once again, the uncertainty might be real or pretended.

Example 15.2.8
We can only wonder whether the participants knew that their negotiations were being tape recorded.

Exercise 15.2.1
Rewrite the following sentences, converting each from a declaration or question to an expression of doubt, following the hint given in parentheses.

Example sentence: We should not change over to the new software. (unsure)
Example conversion: I am not so sure we should change over to the new software.

    (a) Who was most content: the child in the swing, the woman on the porch, or the man in the garden? (cannot say)
    (b) Those who did not vote probably wish they had now. (wonder)

15.3 Apophasis.

Apophasis (uh POF uh sis) brings up a subject by pretending not to bring it up. Its legitimate use is to call attention to something briefly, mentioning the existence of an idea without going into it.

Example 15.3.1
I will not mention Houdini's books on magic, nor the tricks he invented, nor his well-known escapes, because I want to focus on the work he did exposing swindlers and cheats.

Example 15.3.2
Andrea has led the breakfast foods division to a double-digit increase in market share; she has coordinated the worldwide advertising campaign for Drizzlies; and she has done more for team-building at corporate than many other VPs. And that's to say nothing of her personal modesty and generosity.

A common use for the mention-by-denial approach of apophasis is as a polite reminder.

Example 15.3.3
Nothing need be said here about the nonenergy uses of coal, such as the manufacture of plastics, drugs, and industrial chemicals, for we are all aware of those. The real issue is. . . .

Example 15.3.4

Of course, I do not need to mention that you should bring a Number 2 pencil to the exam.

Unfortunately, apophasis is misused by some demagogues to attack others while pretending to rise above the mud slinging.

Example 15.3.5

I pass over the fact that my opponent is an alcoholic and a high-school drop-out because I refuse to allow personal failures to enter into this campaign.

The example above represents the sort of transparent ploy that makes readers grind their teeth. Be careful, then, that your uses of apophasis are fair and legitimate. The table below lists some example phrases for invoking apophasis.

Example Phrases for Apophasis	
I do not need to mention	Nothing need be said about
I pass over the fact that	There is no need to discuss
I will not bring up	To say nothing about
I will not dwell on	We can overlook
It need not be mentioned	You do not need to be reminded

Exercise 15.3.1

Write sentences based on the information given, and present each idea in the form of apophasis.

Example information: The budget deficit and continuing losses from sales.

Example sentence: I do not need to mention the budget deficit or the continuing losses from sales.

(a) Bring warm clothing to the winter resort in the mountains.

(b) This new computer system is more fun than the one we use now.

15.4 Anacoluthon.

Anacoluthon (an uh kuh LOO thun) is a sentence whose two pieces do not fit together grammatically. That is, the writer begins a sentence and changes from one sentence construction to another halfway through. When intentional, anacoluthon produces the effect of a sudden change of mind by the writer, captured on paper. The result is a sense of immediacy, that the reader is right there with the writer as the prose is being constructed.

Example 15.4.1

Suddenly we heard an explosion from the direction of the hut. I turned to see the windows blowing out and the roof coming off. I began to—we were all knocked down.

Example 15.4.2

Some rhetoricians believe that anacoluthon has no place in formal or even semiformal prose, but you must use your own judgment. After all, ineffectively used, this device can—well, you have been cautioned enough.

Example 15.4.3

The reasoning behind the move seems to be this. We will make more money by cutting the sales force because the product sells itself. But we need to make these cuts because we aren't selling enough products. So if we cut, we will gain even though we—this makes no sense at all.

Anacoluthon can be used literarily to reflect confusion or the grasping thinking of an uncertain speaker.

Example 15.4.4

We started out going north on the—it was hot that day, because—then that animal came into the clearing where it—Petey saw it, too—and I turned, but I fell. And, and now I'm here.

Exercise 15.4.1

In each case below, break off the first sentence at an effective point and insert the second sentence, to create anacoluthon.

Example sentences: The ink is smeared, the colors are faint, the box is glued sloppily. No one will buy this cereal.

Example anacoluthon: The ink is smeared, the colors are faint, the box is—no one will buy this cereal.

(a) The kids were unusually noisy, the classroom felt like an oven, and the playground was muddy. I tell you, my day was a nightmare.

(b) The buffet has crab legs, venison, prime rib, salmon, pork chops, and lots more. I want it all.

Style Check 15: The Levels of Style.

Classical rhetoricians identified three levels of style—high, middle, and low—to be used depending on the audience and subject matter. (For example, an epic poem would be written in high style, while a satiric poem might be written in low style.) Today we can think of these styles as levels of formality: formal, semiformal, and familiar. Each style has a purpose, and most people use all three (and shades in between).

Style Check 12 in Chapter 12 describes style as the way something is said. Building on this idea helps distinguish among the levels of style.

Precise diction. The more formal the writing, the more carefully chosen are the words, in order to prevent confusion. Vague words (for example, *many, generally, really, somewhat*) are reduced in favor of more exact words. Slang words and colloquialisms (for example, *the geek was hammered in the tackle*) are avoided in formal writing.

Serious and poised tone. Formal writing usually presents a feeling of respectful seriousness. (See Style Check 16 in Chapter 16 for a further discussion about tone.) Expressions that might indicate an overly casual or overly familiar attitude are avoided. For example, most formal writing avoids the use of contractions (such as *don't, isn't*). Some formal writing arenas do not permit the use of the first person (*I, me*).

Craftsmanship. A formal work of writing requires that sentences be crafted carefully, after a process of thoughtful writing and revising. Formal writing usually contains more subordination and more careful logical structure than informal writing. (A key goal of good style is to learn to write formally without becoming stiff or stuffy.)

Familiar style is often used in personal letters and everyday conversation; semiformal style is common in professional e-mail, memos, and some general business writing; and formal style is preferred for academic, legal, and some business writing. Styles continue to change, and in recent years there has been a move toward less formality in writing. Many nonfiction trade books, for example, are now being written in a semiformal rather than a formal style.

Review Questions.

1. Match the rhetorical device with the appropriate example.

_____ Has anyone seen my blue—never mind; I found them.

_____ The results of the previous attempt need not be brought up. We all remember them.

_____ If no one has read the assignment, how can we have a profitable discussion?

_____ Both of these analyses offer good, but opposite, proposals. I do not know which to choose.

A. rhetorical question

B. aporia

C. apophasis

D. anacoluthon

2. Match the rhetorical device with the appropriate hint.

_____ You do not mention it.

_____ You do not answer it.

_____ You do not finish it.

_____ You do not know it.

A. rhetorical question

B. aporia

C. apophasis

D. anacoluthon

3. Aporia is useful for all of the following except which one?

A. present alternatives without favoring any

B. hide one's ignorance without getting caught

C. politely cast doubt on an idea

D. introduce alternatives for further discussion

4. Rhetorical question is a form of hypophora.

A. True

B. False

5. Which writing task will be the most likely to call for a semiformal style?

A. a research paper written for an upper-division university course

B. an e-mail from one close friend to another

C. a law-school admission essay that "tells us who you are"

Notes

Chapter 16
Word Play

There are those who have called style the image of the writer, for a writer is but his mind . . . and his manner of utterance the very fabric of his ideas. . . .
—Adapted from George Puttenham, *The Arte of English Poesie*

This chapter presents several devices involving words at play. Using one of these devices often provokes a smile from readers, but the use goes far beyond mere amusement. Oxymoron can capture a complex truth with striking effectiveness; a pun can add richness to discourse; and anthimeria can produce a highly memorable statement.

16.1 Oxymoron.

An oxymoron (ok si MŌR on) is a condensed paradox, usually reduced to two words. (A paradox, you will recall, is an *apparent* contradiction that may nevertheless be true or appropriate in some way.)

Example 16.1.1

Wolf whimpers and scratches to be picked up, but when I pick him up, he turns his head away as if he doesn't care that he's being held. It's clearly a case of clinging aloofness.

In the example above, *clinging aloofness* is an oxymoron because the two ideas seem to be contradictory. At the same time, they aptly describe the dog's behavior.

Oxymorons can be divided into two basic types. The first type presents a true paradox, where the terms are logically in tension with each other. The terms *expensive economy* and *helpful useless program* in the examples below are clearly paradoxical.

Example 16.1.2

The cost-saving program, with its layoffs and write-downs, became an expensive economy.

Example 16.1.3

The *Times* has attacked this program as useless. If that is true, it is the most dramatically helpful useless program in the county's history.

In the second type of oxymoron, the writer creates a rhetorical paradox, where ideas that are not normally viewed as contradictory are asserted to be in conflict. In such cases, the writer usually calls attention to this claim. When attention is called to words as words, the words are usually italicized.

Example 16.1.4
With the fare wars putting pressure on the airlines to cut costs wherever they can, the term *airline food* has become an oxymoron.

In this example, there is no natural paradox between the words *airline* and *food*, but the writer declares them to be in conflict: Costs have been cut so much that the poor quality meals served on the airlines can no longer legitimately be called food.

Example 16.1.5
The latchkey child problem, where young children are home alone for lengthy periods—or roaming around outside for hours unsupervised—certainly makes us think the concept of *parental guidance* must be a contradiction in terms.

Here, the writer has deemed the common phrase *parental guidance* an oxymoron in order to comment on the lack of parenting in some situations.

Two-word oxymorons are usually created either in an adjective-noun relationship or an adverb-adjective relationship.

Example 16.1.6
Adjective-noun oxymoron: He was now sufficiently composed to order a funeral of modest magnificence, suitable [to] . . . the reputation of his wealth. —Samuel Johnson

Example 16.1.7
Adverb-adjective oxymoron: When the war ended, the man the Soviets thought to have been a valuable counterspy turned out to have been treacherously loyal to the United States, after all.

Even though two-word oxymorons in the styles above are the most common, short phrases may contain oxymorons, also. In the examples below, *attack of peace* and *pride in his humility* are short-phrase oxymorons because of their paradoxical sense.

Example 16.1.8
The conflict was ended abruptly by an attack of peace, spearheaded by the relief workers.

Example 16.1.9
He takes too much pride in his humility for me to think him truly modest.

Oxymorons that are also alliterative (see Chapter 14, Section 14.1), such as *modest magnificence* in Example 16.1.6 above, can be especially effective.

Exercise 16.1.1

In each case below, label the oxymoron with a *T* if it is a true paradox (an apparent logical contradiction) or with an *R* if it is a rhetorical paradox (a phrase that a writer might claim to involve a logical contradiction, but which otherwise does not).

    (a) sad joy

    (b) wise fool

    (c) military intelligence

    (d) tender cruelty

    (e) speeding slowly

    (f) government efficiency

    (g) noisy silence

    (h) cat owner

    (i) despairing hope

    (j) temporary tax

Exercise 16.1.2

Write a sentence containing an oxymoron according to each instruction below.

    (a) Write a sentence about criminals who stage accidents in order to cheat insurance companies. Use a phrase that shows that the accident is no accident.

    (b) Write a sentence containing the rhetorical oxymoron *weather forecast*, claiming that it is a contradiction in terms.

16.2 Pun.

A pun plays with the multiple meanings of a word or words. One word may be used in a way that suggests several meanings, or two words that sound alike (or almost alike) may be used, with their different meanings. Silly puns have in modern times reduced the pun to its current status as "the lowest form of humor," but historically puns were often considered witty and elegant because they were often well done.

Example 16.2.1

    Thou still unravish'd bride of quietness

    Thou foster child of silence and slow time. . . . —John Keats

When Keats wrote these lines in "Ode on a Grecian Urn," he used the word *still* as a triple pun, meaning, *as of now* (or *yet*), *unmoving*, and *forever*.

As the Keats example demonstrates, one form of pun is to use a word once that can represent two or more different words that are all spelled and pronounced the same (that is, they are homonyms).

Example 16.2.2

Tell me, what's the scoop on cat litter?

Here, *scoop* is a colloquial term for timely information as well as a standard word for a small shovel.

Example 16.2.3

By introducing a camera, we are going to take a shot at the photography business. Let's hope it will be the picture of profitability. After all, digital cameras have no negatives.

In this example, *shot* refers both to a gunshot (*take a shot at*, a metaphor for an attempt) and a photograph (*take a picture*). Similarly, *picture* puns on the pictures that will be taken by the camera and the common metaphor *picture of*, referring to the physical manifestation of some quality (as in *picture of happiness*). And *negatives* puns on the negatives produces by film cameras and *negatives* meaning *disadvantages*.

Sometimes the two words and their meanings are separated.

Example 16.2.4

Do not try to beat the machine. You would be a fool if you tried to fool the lie detector.

In the example above, the word *fool* is first used as a noun (meaning *a naïve or silly person*) and then as a verb (meaning *to deceive*).

Example 16.2.5

Before you charge everything in sight, remember that a long bill takes a long time to pay.

The word *long* in the first use here means *containing many items* (a metaphorical meaning derived from the physical length of a bill with many items), and in the second use means *of extended duration*.

The pun may be implied rather than expressed when the second meaning of the punning word is not stated.

Example 16.2.6

He told me he would come to the dinner tastefully dressed. His suit was great, but if his tie were ice cream, you'd spit it out.

In this case, the sentence puns on the word *taste*, in the two senses of *fashion* and *flavor*. The implication that the tie is in bad taste is made all the more forceful by comparing it with ice cream, which most people find delicious. The idea of ice cream that tastes bad enough to spit out therefore exaggerates the bad (fashion) taste of the tie.

Another type of pun plays upon words that sound the same but have different spellings as well as different meanings (these words are homophonic—they sound the same—but not homographic—they are not spelled the same).

Example 16.2.7

I want to altar my marital status.

Here, the word *altar* is associated with the marriage ceremony because many people are married in front of an altar. The sentence, however, also suggests the expected verb, *alter*, meaning *change*. The use of *altar* (in this case a noun being used as a verb) is also a clever anthimeria (see Section 16.3, later in this chapter). Thus, the sentence, pun included, means, "I want to take my marital status to the altar and alter it."

Example 16.2.8

Travel is down, but so are fuel costs. What effect is this having on profitability? The airlines should give us the plane truth.

This example substitutes the word *plane* (short for *airplane*) for the word that is grammatically expected, *plain*, to create the pun.

Still another type is the allusive pun, where a famous phrase is called to mind by a similar expression. (See the discussion of allusion in Chapter 8, Section 8.1.)

Example 16.2.9

With this season's extra snowfall and the improved economy, lift operators all over the region are exclaiming, "There's no business like snow business."

In the example above, the well-known statement, "There's no business like show business," is echoed, with only a minor change.

Example 16.2.10

County weed abatement crews are razing cane along the shore of the lake.

This example reminds readers of the expression *raising Cain* (an idiom meaning *creating a disturbance* or *acting violently*).

Some puns are created by neologizing. A neologism (nē AHL uh jiz um) is a newly created word. The neologism is frequently a combination of two other words or a formation that suggests one or more other words.

Example 16.2.11

The candle has dripped onto the table. We seem to have had another waxident.

The neologism *waxident* suggests the word *accident* but has combined that word with the substance of a dripped candle: wax. The context allows readers to define *waxident* as "an accident with wax."

Example 16.2.12

They had expected this tragic news to paint an original grief, but the only result was silk-screamed platitudes.

In this example, *silk-screamed* puns on *silk-screened*, a process of mass printing (as on T-shirts) as opposed to the creating of unique, original works of art. Thus, *silk-screamed* implies a less-than-genuine sorrow, as if the expression of sorrow is easily reproduced.

Exercise 16.2.1

In each case below, explain how the pun works.

(a) Here are the two attack robots on tonight's show. The one with the metal shell is Armorgeddon, and the one with the sharp point is Skewer Rat.

(b) He took a trip in the fall—or was it a stumble in the spring?

(c) It is indeed unfortunate to see how much good food goes to waist.

Exercise 16.2.2

Write a sentence containing a pun according to the instructions in each case below.

(a) Pun on words that are spelled the same but that have different meanings, as in Examples 16.2.1 through 16.2.5. Sample words are *pitch, arms, point*. (Hint: To find possible puns on words with the same spelling, look in the dictionary for words with many definitions.)

(b) Pun on words that are spelled differently but that sound the same, as in Examples 16.2.7 and 16.2.8. Sample words are *fare/fair, guest/guessed, ring/wring*.

16.3 Anthimeria.

Anthimeria (an thi MER ē uh) uses one part of speech as if it were another. The most common form of anthimeria is the use of a noun as if it were a verb.

Example 16.3.1

I can keyboard that article this afternoon.

Example 16.3.2

That proposal was river-bottomed long ago.

Example 16.3.3

Friends who Internet together, stay together.

The noun-as-verb use has become so pervasive, in fact, that jokes are made about it:

Example 16.3.4

Don't you hate it when people verb nouns?

When a particular substitution has occurred often enough, the noun actually becomes a verb and is no longer thought of as a substitution. For example, in the expression, "Book the flight," we now understand *book* as a verb, even though it was originally only a noun. The same is also true for the comment, "I'll phone you tomorrow," or even, "E-mail me or fax me instead." Because so many nouns are now used as verbs, your use should be unusual if you want it to stand out.

Example 16.3.5

The goal of the modern tourist is not the experience of the grand journey, nor even the stimulation of meeting a different people. The goal of the modern tourist is to find a scene that will camera well.

In this example, the substitution of *camera* for the verb *photograph* emphasizes the mechanics of taking the picture over the picture itself. The writer appears to imply that what looks good through the viewfinder not only is more important than the scene but also more important than a photograph of the scene. (Of course, *photograph* itself was once only a noun but became a verb as well through anthimeria. In the early days of photography, people used to say, "Let's make a picture" or "Let's take a photograph.")

The other relatively common substitution is the use of some other part of speech in place of a noun. An adjective is a familiar substitute.

Example 16.3.6

When the tourists saw the painted carvings, many bought the red, but few bought the blue.

Here, *many* is an adjective substituting for *many of them* or *many tourists*, *red* is an adjective substituting for *red ones* or *red carvings*, and so on with *few* and *blue*. Such a familiar use, however, creates no special effect. To highlight an idea, the anthimeria must be unusual, as in the following example.

Example 16.3.7

The children ran down the walk, across the beach, and into the foaming wet.

In the example above, the adjective *wet* is used in place of a noun (*ocean* or *water*). Some of the other possible substitutions are shown in the examples below.

Example 16.3.8

Adverb as noun: I've looked all through the proposal, but I can't find the when anywhere.

Example 16.3.9

Preposition as adjective: The across viewpoint is in error.

Example 16.3.10

Adjective as verb: The doctor aloofed the nurse's friendly greeting.

Example 16.3.11

Verb as noun: The designer thought it over, and three imagines later, the proposed product looked completely different.

Exercise 16.3.1

Write sentences containing anthimeria according to the following instructions for each.

(a) Use the noun *cattle prod* as a verb, as in Example 16.3.1, relating to getting a stalled court case moving.

(b) Use the verb *bake* as a noun, as in Example 16.3.11, relating to a hike in the desert.

Style Check 16: Tone.

When you speak, your tone of voice has a substantial effect on the meaning of the words you use. Take a moment to say, "Thanks," in as many different tones of voice as you can. The same word can be perceived by your hearer as sincere, sarcastic, flippant, or deeply felt. You can express a little gratitude or a lot, merely by using the appropriate tone of voice.

Writing also has a tone that provides cues to readers about your attitude and mood. Through the control of diction (choice of words), level of detail, subjects mentioned, kinds of images chosen, and so forth, a tone can be produced that reveals a writer's (or the persona's—see Style Check 13) attitudes:

- The writer's attitude toward the subject (serious, ironic, careless, critical)
- The writer's attitude toward the reader (respectful, condescending, familiar)
- The writer's attitude toward himself or herself (wise, self-deprecating, proud, humble)
- The writer's attitude toward the world and values (cynical, optimistic, paranoid, superior, nihilistic, affirming)

When you approach your subject or think about your audience, consider the tone you want to create. When you choose your metaphors or other rhetorical devices, think about the effect they will have on your tone. How will this or that word or image affect the perceived attitude you have toward your subject or your reader?

Review Questions.

1. Match the rhetorical device with the appropriate example.

   _____ Like many decorators, she could not bear to see bare walls.

   _____ There is too much slowly in this plan: We must move fast.

   _____ The tragic ending to the film gave her the happy sorrow she so much enjoyed.

   A. oxymoron

   B. pun

   C. anthimeria

2. Which is **not** one of the two kinds of oxymoron discussed in the chapter?

   A. false paradox

   B. rhetorical paradox

   C. true paradox

3. A pun can play upon

   A. two or more meanings of one word.

   B. the meanings of two different words that sound the same.

   C. the use of one word that suggests another word.

   D. any of the above.

4. In the following examples, all of the underlined nouns-as-verbs are now common verbs **except** which one?

   A. Land the plane.

   B. Table the resolution.

   C. Clock the sprinter.

   D. Coffin the merger.

5. Readers who discern that a writer is being condescending toward them have detected which aspect of the writer's style?

   A. rhythm

   B. texture

   C. tone

Notes

Appendix A: Rhetoric in Context I
Newspaper Editorial

On the following page are two samples of a newspaper editorial, an original and a revised version containing specific rhetorical devices. The added rhetorical devices are underlined in the text and then named and discussed in the notes across the page.

Before you read the version with the rhetorical devices, examine the original version and think about its strengths and weaknesses. Does it communicate clearly and effectively? How would you improve it? You may want to revise it and add some rhetorical devices where you think they would improve the presentation.

When you read the revised version, think about its strengths and weaknesses as well. Is it, overall, more effective than the original? If so, why? What exactly makes it an improvement?

Look at each specific device and think about whether it has been used effectively. Is the usage appropriate? Does the device promote communication or emphasis or clarity? Now compare the revised sentence with the original across the page. In your judgment, is the revision an improvement? Why or why not?

[Original editorial]

Governor's Budget Fiasco

Once again, the governor has proposed a budget that is supposedly balanced even though it contains increased spending while reducing taxes. A closer look, however, shows that this plan is really unworkable.

It is true that the budget balances, yet it relies on speculative events in the state economy rather than on historical revenue predictions. The governor expects the budget to balance because of a stronger economy that will provide more payroll tax and sales tax revenue. He also expects that social services spending will decline as the improved economy allows more people to leave welfare. These expectations are not likely to be met.

The governor's unlikely plan is further complicated by the fact that, even if his expectations relating to revenues and expenditures are met, additional funds will still be needed to balance the budget. The governor plans to obtain these funds by borrowing against the state retirement system and paying the money back in future budget years.

We believe that this budget represents poor accounting practice.

Certainly a more realistic proposal could have been developed, one which would be much more likely to work.

[Revised editorial]

Governor's Budget Fiasco

Once again, the governor has proposed to the legislature a budget that spends more, taxes less, and remains balanced.[1] However, a closer look reveals that what presumably is a politician's dream is in reality an accountant's nightmare.[2]

The budget is balanced, indeed,[3] but not on the basis of historical revenue predictions. Instead, it is balanced on the couch of a dubious dream.[4] The budget will balance, the governor says, because he expects a very optimistically stronger economy with higher payroll tax revenue; he anticipates a double-digit increase in sales tax revenue; and he projects a reduction in social services spending as the welfare rolls decline.[5] Expects, anticipates, projects.[6] Perhaps the words should be imagines, hopes, wishes.[7]

Such a hallucination—no, that's unfair—let's call it optimism.[8] Such optimism is further complicated by the fact that, even if these unrealistic expectations are realized (they have the same chance as any dream of coming true),[9] the budget will still not balance without borrowing against state retirement funds, which someone, sometime in the future, somehow will pay off.[10]

Where did the governor learn accounting, anyway?[11]

We are saddened that this proposal was not thought through for twenty seconds[12] before being presented to its only welcoming audience, the paper shredder.[13]

Explanatory Notes

In the following notes, the numbers in parentheses refer to the chapter and section number discussing the device. For example, 6.2 would mean Chapter 6, Section 6.2.

[1] Parallelism (1.1) and diazeugma (9.2) for clarity and emphasis. The three short, parallel verb phrases (linked diazeugmatically through the relative pronoun *that*) convey the ideas much more clearly than the original. The reader grasps the facts of the governor's proposal immediately.

[2] Antithesis (1.3) for emphasis and contrast. The metaphors (6.3) of *dream* and *nightmare* produce vivid and powerful images, lacking in the original's use of *unworkable*.

[3] Expletive (2.4) to emphasize the *balanced, but* idea. A *however* or *nevertheless* would have been even stronger than *but*.

[4] Personification (7.3) and alliteration (14.1) for visual effect and memorability. Dreams are in themselves unreliable, and to add a further qualifier, *dubious*, makes the point even more firmly. The alliterated phrase *dubious dream* has enough memorability that readers may recall it after reading the editorial, as a summing up of the writer's position. A phrase that can encapsulate a position may border on sloganeering, but it can also serve as an aid to memory.

[5] Parallelism (1.1) with three sentences using the same syntax. The anaphora (11.1) repeating *he* emphasizes that these are the governor's ideas and not necessarily anyone else's. The editorial writer is here isolating the governor's ideas in order to attack them (and him) personally.

[6] Asyndeton (2.2) to imply that the governor may indulge other such verbs. The listing of just the verbs invites the reader to consider them in isolation, to see that they represent desired rather than definite future states.

[7] Asyndeton (2.2) again, creating an antithesis (1.3) with the previous list, for contrast and correction of the governor's ideas. The writer implies that these words, describing an even less definite future, are actually more applicable to the governor's ideas than the ones he used.

[8] Metanoia (5.4) to present a strong term, *hallucination*, and then pretend to erase it. The word and its effect remain, of course, set in print. When the writer decides to *call it optimism*, the sense of *call it* implies that the writer is changing words only to be polite, as if (with a wink at the reader) a euphemism for the real thing (perhaps not quite a hallucination, but not really optimism, either) will be substituted out of kindness.

[9] Parenthesis (10.4) to remind the reader of the dream idea while not dropping the main idea of the sentence.

[10] Anaphora (11.1), alliteration (14.1), and hypozeugma (9.5) for emphasis and memorability. Piling up indefinite and vague terms makes the goal of paying off the borrowing seem unrealistic. The terms also imply that the plan itself is not very definite.

[11] Rhetorical question (15.1). The implied answer might be, "I don't know. Maybe nowhere. Maybe at a weak school."

[12] Synecdoche (7.2) with a short time standing for more time, thereby also creating understatement (3.2).

[13] Personification (7.3) for effect and appositive (10.3) to create the surprise effect with the most emphasis at the end of the sentence.

Exercise A.1

Revise the following editorial, improving its effectiveness by adding at least three rhetorical devices. Underline and label each device.

Parking Proposal Not Needed

At its regular meeting last night, the City Council proposed to install new, electronic parking meters in the downtown area. These meters, unlike the ones in use now, will "zero out" the moment a car leaves the spot, regardless of the time left on the meter.

As a result, there will be no more "free time" for lucky drivers when the previous driver leaves some time. For many downtown drivers, a few minutes free is the only thing they can hope for in an otherwise difficult parking environment.

The council members say this change will produce additional revenue. However, no one mentioned how much money might be made. After all, the new meters are expensive. Just paying for them would take a long time. The city would not receive any net revenue until the meters were paid off. The meter manufacturer must have some good salesmen.

We urge the council to reconsider this ill-advised move.

Appendix B: Rhetoric in Context II
Business Memorandum

On the following page are two samples of a business memorandum, an original and a revised version containing specific rhetorical devices. The added rhetorical devices are underlined in the text and then named and discussed in the notes across the page.

Before you read the version with the rhetorical devices, examine the original version and think about its strengths and weaknesses. Does it communicate clearly and effectively? How would you improve it? You may want to revise it and add some rhetorical devices where you think they would improve the presentation.

When you read the revised version, think about its strengths and weaknesses as well. Is it, overall, more effective than the original? If so, why? What exactly makes it an improvement?

Look at each specific device and think about whether it has been used effectively. Is the usage appropriate? Does the device promote communication or emphasis or clarity? Now compare the revised sentence with the original across the page. In your judgment, is the revision an improvement? Why or why not?

[Original memorandum]

To: Metro Managers
From: Gloria Lopez, VP Marketing
Subj.: Overnight Inventory for Category 3 Books

Beginning January 1, all metro locations of Barnaby's will change the display model for Category 3 books. Instead of shelving three copies of each book, stores will shelve one. In order to maintain the availability of books that sell, point-of-sale information will be sent to the shipping department, and another copy of each sold book will ship to the store the next day.

It is expected that the reduction of the number of copies of slow-selling titles will open shelf space. As a result, we expect to sell more books because we can display more different ones. We also hope to reduce inventory costs.

Last year the metro stores received nearly 60,000 customer requests for current but unstocked books. Also, 74 percent of our customers purchased multiple books when they bought something. If we can put more books in front of our customers, they will buy more of them. We are here to serve our customers, who want a wider selection.

[Revised memorandum]

To: Metro Managers
From: Gloria Lopez, VP Marketing
Subj.: Overnight Inventory for Category 3 Books

Beginning January 1, all metro locations of Barnaby's will change the display model for Category 3 (that is, backlist slow-seller)[1] books. The change[2] will involve a reduction in shelving, from three copies of each title to one copy each.[3] In order to maintain the availability of books that sell, point-of-sale information will alert the central warehouse,[4] and another copy of each sold title will ship to the store the next day.

Why are we doing this?[5] Reducing the number of copies of slow-selling titles will open shelf space. As a result, we expect to display more titles, sell more books, and reduce inventory costs.[6]

Last year the metro stores had almost sixty thousand do-you-haves[7] for current but unstocked books. And importantly,[8] 74 percent of our customers purchased multiple titles when they bought books. The more words we can put in front of their eyes,[9] the more sales we will get. We are here to serve our customers. Selection they demand and selection we will have.[10]

Explanatory Notes

In the following notes, the numbers in parentheses refer to the chapter and section number discussing the device. For example, 6.2 would mean Chapter 6, Section 6.2.

[1] Distinctio (5.1) for clarification of a term that is not self-explanatory. A quick reminder of the term's meaning makes the memo easier to negotiate.

[2] Conduplicatio (12.2), pulling out the word *change* from the previous sentence and highlighting it by putting it at the beginning of the next. This creates not only a clarifying focus, but also a good transition for continuity of thought.

[3] Parallelism (1.1) for clarity. Note that *title* is technically a synecdoche (7.2), but it is so commonly used that it is no longer noted as a metaphorical usage.

[4] Metonymy (7.1), substituting *warehouse* in place of "the appropriate people who work in the shipping department at the warehouse." Note how much more condensed, clear, and effective rhetoric can be.

[5] Hypophora (4.3) to answer an expected question. Whenever a change is made, people want to know why. The question could have been answered without asking it ("We are doing this because"), but expressing the question helps bring readers into the discussion. Those who thought of the question will think, "My question exactly," while those who did not will have their curiosity raised by it.

[6] Diazeugma (9.2) and parallelism (1.1) for clarity and emphasis. Putting the verb phrases together in this abbreviated, parallel form makes the sequential logic of the plan more apparent: display, sell, reduce.

[7] Anthimeria (16.3). Instead of using the word *questions*, the writer substitutes the familiar part of the question itself, using it as a noun, to emphasize that these are the requests coming from prospective buyers (in their own words). Every manager or employee would like to answer a "do you have" with a Yes. The anthimeria itself is unusual enough to gain extra notice. Note the difference in impact between the statements, "We get lots of questions" and, "We get lots of do-you-haves." The latter is much more specific and immediate.

[8] Expletive (2.4) to stress the importance of the statistics.

[9] Synecdoche (7.2), substituting *words in front of eyes* for *books*. It is the words that people read. The use of the critical-part-for-whole reminds the managers that people like to browse books and read a little here and there before buying them. So, it is, in a sense, literally true that the more words (from many books) put in front of prospective buyers, the more sales will probably result.

[10] Hyperbaton (10.1) and anaphora (11.1) combined, emphasizing the idea of improved selection, which is a substantial part of the new policy. The writer saves the most unusual device (a dramatic change in syntax) for the end, where being overtly rhetorical adds a flourish that implies, "The memo is now concluded." The unusual wording also provides something memorable for the readers to connect with the content of the memo. If someone should ask, "What was the memo about?" the writer may hope that the manager can reply, "Selection they demand and selection we will have."

Exercise B.1
Revise the following business memorandum, improving its effectiveness by adding at least three rhetorical devices. Underline and label each device you use.

To: All Association Managers

From: Pat Olley, VP Customer Relations

Re: Guaranteed Contractors

According to recent surveys, a major concern of both our homeowners association board members and the residents of our associations is that of finding a reliable contractor to do work for them individually. Many members appear to fear that contractors all too often will overcharge them. Sometimes the work is of questionable quality.

To address this concern, Triangle Property Management has developed a list of contractors who have proven reliable in their services in the past. They also have agreed to guarantee their work. Any disputes will be settled through arbitration with a TPM associate.

Please inform your board members at their next meeting that we will be happy to distribute this list with their approval. It is our hope that our association residents will no longer feel so lost when they need to choose a contractor.

Appendix C: Rhetoric in Context III
Social Worker's Report About a Client

On the following page are two samples of a social worker's report about a client, an original and a revised version containing specific rhetorical devices. The added rhetorical devices are underlined in the text and then named and discussed in the notes across the page.

Before you read the version with the rhetorical devices, examine the original version and think about its strengths and weaknesses. Does it communicate clearly and effectively? How would you improve it? You may want to revise it and add some rhetorical devices where you think they would improve the presentation.

When you read the revised version, think about its strengths and weaknesses as well. Is it, overall, more effective than the original? If so, why? What exactly makes it an improvement?

Look at each specific device and think about whether it has been used effectively. Is the usage appropriate? Does the device promote communication or emphasis or clarity? Now compare the revised sentence with the original across the page. In your judgment, is the revision an improvement? Why or why not?

[Original report]

Mrs. Wallace is a 54-year-old, widowed cashier. When her husband died three years ago, Mrs. Wallace was left alone to care for her 78-year-old invalid mother. Before her husband's death, Mrs. Wallace had not worked outside the home, so when it became necessary for her to work, she was qualified only for a low-paying job as a cashier.

She contacted the social worker because she feels overwhelmed, powerless, and threatened. Her mother's health is deteriorating, she is feeling financial pressure, and her employer is upset about the number of hours she has missed recently, caused by her need to take her mother to the doctor or emergency room.

Mrs. Wallace expressed frustration with her job and her lot in life, saying that caring for her mother left her no time to take some courses that would qualify her for a better job. She has thought of training to be a bookkeeper. She repeatedly expressed her love for her mother and said she feels guilty even thinking about not caring for her.

I reassured Mrs. Wallace that I would become her advocate and her ally in helping her solve these problems. I told her that we would identify each problem and work on one at a time. We discussed the possibility of alternative caregivers who could be her mother's companions while Mrs. Wallace went to class. She might be agreeable to this idea.

[Revised report]

Mrs. Wallace is a 54-year-old, widowed cashier. When her husband died three years ago, Mrs. Wallace was left alone to care for her mother, _now a 78-year-old invalid._[1] _Before her husband's death, Mrs. Wallace had not worked outside the home, so when work became necessary, she was qualified only for a low-paying job as a cashier._[2]

She contacted the social worker because she feels _overwhelmed and powerless and threatened._[3] Her mother's health is deteriorating, she is feeling financial pressure, and her employer is _not at all happy_[4] about the number of hours she has missed recently, caused by her need to take her mother to the doctor or emergency room.

Mrs. Wallace revealed a _crushed and trampled_[5] spirit: _Her job, her lot in life, her mother's care, and her lack of personal time were all mentioned_[6] as sources of frustration. Caring for her mother has left her no time to take some courses that would qualify her for a _good, good_[7] job. She has thought of training to be a bookkeeper. She repeatedly expressed her love for her mother and said she feels guilty even thinking about not caring for her.

I reassured Mrs. Wallace that I would become her advocate and her ally in _drawing up a blueprint_[8] to help her solve these problems. I told her that we would identify each problem and work on one at a time. We discussed the possibility of volunteer caregivers, _such as church friends,_[9] who could be her mother's companions while Mrs. Wallace went to class. _It is unclear whether this idea will be accepted._[10]

Explanatory Notes

In the following notes, the numbers in parentheses refer to the chapter and section number discussing the device. For example, 6.2 would mean Chapter 6, Section 6.2.

[1] Appositive (10.3), allowing the clear phrase *caring for her mother* to make its point before modifying it with a description of age and health. Placing the word *invalid* at the end of the sentence further emphasizes the problem of care.

[2] Conduplicatio (12.2) to pull out the idea of work from the previous clause.

[3] Polysyndeton (2.3) to create the effect of an overwhelming piling on of troubles and frustrations that Mrs. Wallace feels. This use is especially effective here for creating a sense that Mrs. Wallace feels attacked from every direction.

[4] Litotes (3.3) to emphasize the employer's negative feelings. In the original, calling the employer *upset* has a lesser effect. We assume that being upset to some degree is expected. On the other hand, *not at all happy* implies a greater degree of dissatisfaction, perhaps even anger.

[5] Onomatopoeia (14.2) to reflect the sounds of damage. There is also an implied metaphor (6.3) here, where Mrs. Wallace's spirit is being compared to something that can be trampled underfoot or crushed in a press (or perhaps under a wheel).

[6] Hypozeugma (9.5) to provide clarity to the list and anaphora (11.1) to emphasize the *her*. Note how the use of a zeugmatic device (Chapter 9) helps to set up an orderly, understandable list. Compare this easily graspable list with the first sentence of the third paragraph of the original report, and you can see the difference.

[7] Epizeuxis (13.2) for emphasis. The original has *a better job*, but Mrs. Wallace clearly wants to move into a *much* better job, one that she will think of as good. The social worker may have used this expression with Mrs. Wallace. Instead of saying, "I'll help you get a better job," she might have said, "I'll help you get a good, good job." See the difference?

[8] Metaphor (6.3) to provide a visual and concrete image. *Plan* is very abstract, while *blueprint* is visual, and includes the positive connotation of construction and newness.

[9] Exemplum (5.2) to supply a specific example of what was discussed. The concept of volunteer caregiver is made clearer by even one concrete example.

[10] Aporia (15.2) to indicate caution. The social worker has at least some doubt that the proposed solution will be acceptable to her client.

Exercise C.1
Revise the following social worker's report, improving its effectiveness by adding at least three rhetorical devices. Underline and label each device you use.

Jennifer is an 18-year-old freshman at a first-rank private university. Her father attended the same school. Her father is now divorced and has put his hopes of success in his daughter. He wants her to follow his career choice and become a medical doctor. He has announced that he will not permit her to fail.

Jennifer sought the social worker's help because she has been suffering from insomnia, panic attacks, self-doubt, nightmares (when she does sleep), and anxiety. Even though she earned A's in high school, she has found the university to be substantially more challenging, and she fears failing. She feels conflicted because her father wants her to be a doctor, even though she would like to study art or architecture.

I reassured her that she was not alone in her concerns. I told her there were many possible solutions. I urged her to have a talk with her father about her own aspirations. I also put her in contact with the Study Skills Center for help with time management. She appeared relieved at the end of our session.

Appendix D: Rhetoric in Context IV
Graduate School Application Essay

On the following page are two sample excerpts of a graduate school application essay, an original and a revised version containing specific rhetorical devices. The added rhetorical devices are underlined in the text and then named and discussed in the notes across the page.

Before you read the version with the rhetorical devices, examine the original version and think about its strengths and weaknesses. Does it communicate clearly and effectively? How would you improve it? You may want to revise it and add some rhetorical devices where you think they would improve the presentation.

When you read the revised version, think about its strengths and weaknesses as well. Is it, overall, more effective than the original? If so, why? What exactly makes it an improvement?

Look at each specific device and think about whether it has been used effectively. Is the usage appropriate? Does the device promote communication or emphasis or clarity? Now compare the revised sentence with the original across the page. In your judgment, is the revision an improvement? Why or why not?

[Original excerpt of essay]

I want to go to law school because I believe that, as an attorney, I can make a positive difference in the lives of others. Many obstacles to a better life are physical or economic, but inadequate or poor legislation causes others. The right laws can go a long way toward removing obstacles to success. My ultimate goal is to become a legislator or jurist so that I can play a role in improving the legal environment of my city, state, or nation.

My part-time jobs have given me experience as an employee of many aspects of business law, and, as a major in economics, I believe that my theoretical understanding of business will prepare me well for my studies in corporate law. My love of debate and participation on the debate team will help prepare me for the courtroom. I have won several trophies at speech contests. Further, I know that attorneys must write substantial amounts of prose, so I have taken extra writing courses while here at State.

While pursuing my studies and working part-time as an assistant manager in a bookstore, I also have held leadership positions in student government.

I am well trained and experienced to be motivated to pursue my desire to succeed in law school. I want to become known as a great public servant, who made a difference in the lives of others.

[Revised excerpt of essay]

I want to go to law school because I believe that, as an attorney, I can make a difference—a substantial difference[1]—in the lives of others. Physical and economic hardships produce many obstacles to a better life, but in many other cases those obstacles are laws,[2] laws inadequate to meet the needs of a changing society.[3] Law should remove the barriers to success, not become those barriers.[4] My ultimate goal is to become a legislator or jurist so that I can play a role in improving the legal environment of my city, my state, my nation.[5]

My part-time jobs[6] have given me an employee's eye view[7] of many aspects of business law; my major in economics has provided a theoretical understanding of business operations and corporate law; and my participation on the debate team (I have won several trophies at speech contests)[8] has helped to prepare me for those courtroom battles[9] so powerfully presented[10] in Francis Wellman's classic, *The Art of Cross-Examination*.[11] Further, I am certainly[12] aware that attorneys must be sterling crafters of words,[13] so I have taken extra writing courses while here at State.

While pursuing my studies and working part-time as an assistant manager in a bookstore, I also have held leadership positions in student government, including Junior Class treasurer.[14]

My training, experience, and desire for service all motivate me to succeed in law school.[15]

Explanatory Notes

In the following notes, the numbers in parentheses refer to the chapter and section number discussing the device. For example, 6.2 would mean Chapter 6, Section 6.2.

[1] Amplification (5.3) for emphasis, and to avoid the cliché sound of *make a difference* by itself.

[2] Chiasmus (1.2), reversing the parallelism and putting *laws* at the end of the clause for emphasis, and to construct the device that follows.

[3] Anadiplosis (12.1) to emphasize the point that the laws are at fault. *Laws inadequate* may be interpreted as anastrophe (10.2), or it may be seen as an elliptical construction, reading, "laws (that are) inadequate to meet the needs of a changing society." (Relative pronoun clauses beginning with *that are* frequently drop those words, but they remain understood.)

[4] Antithesis (1.3) to make a strong, contrasting point.

[5] Anaphora (11.1) and asyndeton (2.2) to emphasize that the writer is feeling community with all people, whether local, state, or national. The repeated use of *my* shows a feeling of affiliation. The asyndeton is for dramatic effect.

[6] This sentence contains several overlapping devices. Note the parallelism (1.1) in the sentences beginning with *my part-time job, my major in economics,* and *my participation on the debate team.* Compare the original with the revised sentence, and you should see how much clearer and more effective the parallel construction makes the presentation. Note also that the parallelism is not at all strict: The last sentence continues on with modification, making it longer than the other two.

[7] Metonymy (7.1), substituting *eye view* for *understanding* or *experience.* The metaphor is more visual than the word *experience,* which is highly abstract.

[8] Parenthesis (10.4) to add a specific extra honor without stopping the flow of the main idea. In the original, the statement seems almost tacked on. Here, it appears where its presence is most effective.

[9] Metaphor (6.3). The battle metaphor is not fresh or original, but it is still probably superior to "will prepare me for the courtroom" in the original.

[10] Alliteration (14.1) for dramatic and emphatic effect.

[11] Allusion (8.1) to a famous classic in legal writing. Note how such an allusion helps create the impression of being knowledgeable and well read.

[12] Expletive (2.4) to emphasize the entire sentence. Because only one sentence is devoted to the writing issue, the writer emphasizes it with the expletive. The stress also keeps the sentence from appearing to be tacked on as an afterthought.

[13] Metaphor (6.3) to add some life and visual quality to the idea. Compare that to the original's "must write substantial amounts of prose."

[14] Exemplum (5.2) to add some specific detail to an otherwise vague statement.

[15] Hypozeugma (9.5) to present several motivating factors at once.

Exercise D.1

Revise the following excerpt from a graduate school application essay, improving its effectiveness by adding at least three rhetorical devices. Underline and label each device.

I am applying to your graduate program in forensic science because I have always been interested in how crimes are committed and then solved. As a child, I read the Sherlock Holmes stories. I read murder mysteries in high school. In college, my recreational reading has included books about arson investigation, crime-scene searching, and autopsies related to cause-of-death investigations. I love a challenge, and look forward to a career solving challenging crimes.

My major in chemistry has prepared me for studies about toxicology and drug analysis, and I have taken a course in human anatomy to prepare me for further study relating to the body. Many of my courses have emphasized the scientific method.

For the past two years, I have had a part-time job at a pharmacy. There, I have tried to learn as much as possible about the effects of various medicines. I have learned how legal medicines are sometimes abused, and even a little about poisoning, all from a practical point of view.

I believe my academic preparation and my lifelong interest in forensic science will enable me to succeed in your program and to become a valuable asset to solving crimes.

Appendix E: Rhetoric in Context V
Short Story

On the following page are two samples of a short story, an original and a revised version containing specific rhetorical devices. The added rhetorical devices are underlined in the text and then named and discussed in the notes across the page.

Before you read the version with the rhetorical devices, examine the original version and think about its strengths and weaknesses. Does it communicate clearly and effectively? How would you improve it? You may want to revise it and add some rhetorical devices where you think they would improve the presentation.

When you read the revised version, think about its strengths and weaknesses as well. Is it, overall, more effective than the original? If so, why? What exactly makes it an improvement?

Look at each specific device and think about whether it has been used effectively. Is the usage appropriate? Does the device promote communication or emphasis or clarity? Now compare the revised sentence with the original across the page. In your judgment, is the revision an improvement? Why or why not?

[Original short story]

A young man in the prime of life acquired a large amount of possessions, but he was not happy. So he acquired two or three times more. And yet, regardless of how much money he had in the bank, he still felt empty and sad.

Because this is a fable, the obvious solution was to seek wisdom from an all-wise guru. So, the man climbed a steep and difficult mountain. Eventually, he found a hunched-over Wise One sitting on the top.

"Oh, proverbially antiquated one," he began, "I cannot find happiness or contentment. I double my possessions, but no matter how much I own, I still feel empty and sad."

"Solution path fixation," said the seated figure, in a strangely treble voice. "You need to alter your problem-solving dynamic and implement an alternate path to your goal state. Try giving instead of taking as the source of your strategy."

"Excuse me," said the man, "but you speak oddly for an unlearned hermit."

"That's because your expectations are controlling your perceptions," said his newly found adviser, now shaking her black tresses and turning to him. "I'm not a guru at all. I'm a VP of marketing for nonmetallic catheters."

"Hey, you're beautiful. I think I love you. Will you marry me?"

"I suppose I should return your male cliché with the female stereotype: 'Hey, you're rich. I think I love you, too.' But if you don't mind, I'll pass."

"But this is a fairy tale with plot demands, and we're near the end."

"Oh, all right then."

And so they lived happily ever after.

[Revised short story]

A young man in the prime of life acquired <u>enough wealth to fill a blimp hangar,</u>[1] but he was not happy. So he multiplied it. And yet, regardless of <u>the number of zeroes behind the numerals in his bank book,</u>[2] he still felt empty and sad.

Because this is a fable, the obvious solution was to seek <u>the voice of Athena</u>[3] from an all-wise guru. <u>So, the man slowly climbed a steep and difficult mountain and eventually found a hunched-over Wise One sitting on the top.</u>[4]

"Oh, proverbially antiquated one," he began, "I cannot find happiness or contentment. <u>I add exponents to my riches,</u>[5] but no matter how much I own, I still feel <u>(as it says above)</u>[6] empty and sad."

"Solution path fixation," said the seated figure, in a strangely <u>musical</u>[7] voice. "You need to alter your problem-solving dynamic and implement an alternate path to your goal state. <u>Try *give* instead of *get* as the axis of your strategy.</u>"[8]

"Excuse me," said the man, "but you speak oddly for an <u>unlettered</u>[9] hermit."

"That's because your expectations are controlling your perceptions," said his newly found adviser, now shaking her <u>raven</u>[10] tresses and turning to him. "<u>In fact,</u>[11] I'm not a guru at all. I'm a VP of marketing for nonmetallic catheters."

"Hey, you're beautiful. I think I love you. Will you marry me?"

"I suppose <u>I should play Echo</u>[12] to your male cliché with the female stereotype: 'Hey, you're rich. I think I love you, too.' But if you don't mind, I'll pass."

"But this is a fairy tale with plot demands, and we're near the end."

"Oh, all right then."

And so they lived happily ever after.

Explanatory Notes

In the following notes, the numbers in parentheses refer to the chapter and section number discussing the device. For example, 6.2 would mean Chapter 6, Section 6.2.

[1] Metaphor (6.3) to provide a visual element and the sense of largeness. Note how relatively ineffective expressions such as *large amount* are. There is nothing visual for the reader to hang onto. In a longer story, synecdoches could be substituted: "He acquired too many castles and treasure rooms and diamond rings and aromatherapy candles."

[2] Metonymy (7.1), substituting something associated with a large amount of money for the amount. The number with many zeroes also gives a visual sense to the wealth because the reader can imagine a bank book with a large number printed in it.

[3] Eponym (8.2) to refer to wisdom in terms of the words of the goddess of wisdom. Not only does this eponym create a visual substitute for the idea of wisdom, but it also invokes the whole realm of Greek mythology, adding a nice richness to the story.

[4] Parallelism (1.1) and diazeugma (9.2) to emphasize continuity and make the idea flow better.

[5] Metonymy (7.1), where exponents make numbers dramatically larger, and the numbers are associated with the amount of wealth owned.

[6] Parenthesis (10.4) to provide a humorous reference to the story by a character inside the story. (This conscious, internal reference to the story as a story is a metafictional element, as is the reference to plot demands later on.)

[7] Metaphor (6.3) to provide more richness, complexity, and suggestivity than the word *treble* does.

[8] Alliteration (14.1) in a slightly antithetical (1.3) structure, to emphasize the contrast much better than in the original, which uses giving and taking. Additionally, this version uses anthimeria (16.3) by presenting verbs as nouns. This latter use adds brevity and flavor. Finally, *axis* is a metaphor (6.3), providing a more visual appeal than the original's *source*.

[9] Synecdoche (7.2) to produce a more visual and unusual word than *uneducated* or *unlearned*. An alternative synecdoche would be, "You speak oddly for someone who has never seen a book or taken lecture notes."

[10] Metaphor (6.3), or better, a submerged simile (6.1; see Example 6.1.20). While *black* is a visual word, *raven* is much more pictorial because it evokes a specific animal in a definite shade of deep black.

[11] Expletive (2.4) to emphasize the sentence that wheels the plot around.

[12] Allusion (8.1) to the story of Echo, the source of our word *echo*. Once again, mythology can provide some richness without derailing the main story.

Exercise E.1

Revise the following short story, improving its effectiveness by adding at least three rhetorical devices. Underline and label each device you use.

A family drove out to the desert, where they came upon an area with petrified wood. Many of the rocks were colored beautifully, showing patches of brown, red, yellow, and black.

"Pick one to take home for a souvenir," said the father.

"Which should I choose?" his daughter asked, dazzled by the many possibilities.

"The best alternative cannot be selected until you identify, rank, and weight the preferred criteria in your decision-modeling process," her father replied.

"Just choose the prettiest one that's nearby, honey," said her mother, while giving her husband a look.

"I want a heavy one," their son offered, "so I can kill bugs." Soon the boy found a heavy but ugly rock that suited his purpose.

"What about you, dear?" asked the girl's mother.

"Well," the girl replied, "these rocks are all pretty, but I'd really rather have an ice cream cone."

"These are *your* children, you know," said the woman to her husband.

The moral: A choice selects from among the stated alternatives; a wise choice looks beyond them.

Appendix F
Winston Churchill—A Speaker's Rhetoric

Winston Churchill is often described as one of the finest orators of the twentieth century. His speeches helped solidify and encourage British determination to fight against Hitler during World War II. This appendix, divided into two parts, contains examples of Churchill's use of rhetoric in his speeches. Page numbers in parentheses refer to the source text,[1] so that you can examine the excerpts in context, if you want.

Part I. In this part, the devices are underlined to make them easy to find. As a self-test, in the space below each item write the names of the rhetorical devices that Churchill used. Then, check your answers by referring to the Answer Key on the next page of this book.

1. . . . undoubtedly we must measure each case, so far as we can, because our own resources are <u>not unlimited</u>. (679)

2. I listened to his speech with the greatest attention, and both in its assertions and its reservations, <u>in its scope, in its emphasis, and in its balance</u>, I find myself entirely in accord with what he said. (678)

3. When it is known that a powerful confederation of States will infallibly fight—<u>I think it wise to put it in blunt terms</u>—if certain things are done, there are still great hopes and chances that these deeds will not be done. (679)

4. Having begun to create a Grand Alliance against aggression, <u>we cannot afford to fail. We shall be in mortal danger if we fail. We shall be marked down and isolated if we fail.</u> (679)

5. This is <u>a position morally indefensible</u>; moreover, it is a position which lessens the chance of peace. (681)

6. <u>It is like setting up an armoured umbrella</u>, under which other countries can be invited to take shelter as and when they seek to do so. (683)

7. This moral conviction alone affords that ever-fresh resilience which renews the strength and energy of people in long, <u>doubtful and dark days</u>. (693)

8. We have before us <u>many, many</u> long months of struggle and of suffering. (705)

---

[1] Source text: James, R. (1998). *Churchill speaks 1897–1963: Collected speeches in peace & war.* New York: Barnes & Noble. (Original work published 1980.) Reprinted by permission.

Answer Key for Part I of Appendix F

In the following notes, the numbers in parentheses refer to the chapter and section number discussing the device. For example, 6.2 would mean Chapter 6, Section 6.2.

1. Litotes (3.3). Churchill understates the situation because the entire British public was well aware of the shortages of material and supplies at the time.

2. Anaphora (11.1). Churchill repeats *in its* (prepositions and possessive pronouns), not to emphasize them, but to set up the following words. *In its* forms a two-word unstressed pair, so that the words following are necessarily highly stressed.

3. Parenthesis (10.4). The parenthetical statement calls attention to the idea that the British are willing to oppose Hitler in a war, if necessary. (Note also in this sentence the use of epistrophe (11.2) together with antithesis (1.3) to stress, through the *done/not done* contrast, that there was still hope of avoiding war.)

4. Epistrophe (11.2). Churchill repeats the idea of failure, with the later conditional *if*, in order to stress the necessity of a hard effort to avoid failing.

5. Anastrophe (10.2). By delaying the epithet, *indefensible* gains the stress rather than *position*. (Note also the use of anaphora (11.1), repeating *is a position*.)

6. Analogy (6.2). Churchill provides an image that gives visual character to the abstract idea of a military alliance.

7. Alliteration (14.1). Alliteration is useful as an aid to memory. Note how Churchill places the alliteration at the end of the sentence for further emphasis and memorability.

8. Epizeuxis (13.2). World War II, like World War I, lasted for years rather than months.

Part II. Directions: In this part, more than one rhetorical device may be present in each example. As a self-test, underline the device(s) in each one and write the name(s) in the spaces below each item. Then, check your answers by referring to the Answer Key on the next page of this book.

1. . . . the Prime Minister [has declared] . . . that the defence of European freedom and the reign of law constitute causes in which this country will dare all and do all. (678)

2. These are men in the path of whose ambition it is very dangerous to stand, and we have taken up our stand right in their path. (680)

3. It is almost axiomatic that those who are allies of the same Power are allies of one another. It is almost axiomatic. (683)

4. Outside, the storms of war may blow and the lands may be lashed with the fury of its gales, but in our own hearts this Sunday morning, there is peace. Our hands may be active, but our consciences are at rest. (693)

5. Up to the present, time has been on our side; but time is a changeable ally. He may be with you in one period and against you in another. . . . (701)

6. You ask, what is our aim? I can answer in one word: it is victory, victory at all costs, victory in spite of all terror, victory, however long and hard the road may be; for without victory, there is no survival. (705)

7. Here is where we come to the Navy—and after all, we have a Navy. Some people seem to forget that we have a Navy. We must remind them. (716)

8. In the meantime, there may be raids by parachute troops and attempted descents of airborne soldiers. We should be able to give those gentry a warm reception. (717)

Answer Key for Part II of Appendix F

In the following notes, the numbers in parentheses refer to the chapter and section number discussing the device. For example, 6.2 would mean Chapter 6, Section 6.2.

1. Parallelism (1.1) in *defence of European freedom and the reign of law* and in *dare all and do all*. Alliteration (14.1) in *dare* and *do*. Epistrophe (11.2) in *dare all and do all*.

2. Antimetabole (13.3), reversing the order of path and stand. In addition, stand is used in two somewhat different senses (a metaphorical standing in the way of someone and taking a firm position), producing a mild pun (16.2).

3. Diacope (13.1). Note also the use of a short sentence following a longer one to create emphasis.

4. Metaphor (6.3) where war is compared to a storm. Onomatopoeia (14.2) with the word *lashed*. Antithesis (1.3) between the ideas of war outside vs. peace in our hearts and between hands active vs. consciences at rest. The metaphor of a storm creates a sense of reassurance because all are familiar with storms and the fact that they eventually pass. Similarly, the two balanced antitheses create a sense of things under control. Churchill's words here are deliberately constructed to give reassurance to his audience.

5. Personification (7.3). Churchill is addressing anyone who may still be thinking that Britain can wait things out.

6. Hypophora (4.3). A few sentences earlier, Churchill says, "You ask, what is our policy?" and goes on to answer that it is to wage war. He is using hypophora here to address the obvious questions his audience will have. Also present is amplification (5.3), restating the word *victory* and adding clarifying detail.

7. Epistrophe (11.2) to hammer on the idea of the existence of the British navy. Also parenthesis (10.4), where Churchill interrupts himself to remind his hearers that such a thing does exist.

8. Understatement (3.2), where *a warm reception* will actually be a hot reception. Churchill is also being ironic (3.1) by referring to the enemy soldiers as *gentry*.

Index

abbreviations 42
alliteration 127–130
allusion 73–75
amplification 42–43
anacoluthon 144–145
anadiplosis 111–112
analogy 52–54
anaphora 103–105
anastrophe 94–96
anthimeria 154–156
antimetabole 122–123
antithesis 7–9
apophasis 143–144
aporia 141–143
apostrophe 76–78
appositive 96–97
assonance 133–134
asyndeton 12–14
balance 1
catachresis 58–59
chiasmus 5–7
clarity 1, 39–45
climax 11–12
conduplicatio 112–114
consonance 134–135
cumulative sentence 89–90
diacope 119–120
diazeugma 84–85
distinctio 39–41
duck story 135
elegance 2
epanalepsis 114–115
epistrophe 105–107
epithet, transferred 78–80
epizeuxis 120–122
eponym 75–76
exemplum 41–42
expletive 15–18
freshness 71
hyperbaton 93–94
hyperbole 26
hypophora 33–35
hypotaxis 99–100
hypozeugma 87–88
irony 21–22
litotes 24–25

mesozeugma 86–87
metabasis 29–30
metanoia 43–45
metaphor 54–57, 59–60
metonymy 63–65
neologism 153–154
onomatopoeia 130–132
oxymoron 149–151
parallelism 1–5
parataxis 99–100
parenthesis 98–99
periodic sentence 89–90
persona 80
personification 68–70
polysyndeton 14–15
positioning for emphasis 27
procatalepsis 30–32
prozeugma 85–86
pun 151–154
rhetorical question 139–141
rhythm 2, 9
scesis onomaton 123–124
short sentences 108–109
simile 47–51
stress 18–19
style 115–116, 146
style check
    1: rhythm 9
    2: Demetrius on beginning and ending stress 18–19
    3: emphatic positioning 27
    4: transitions of logic 35–36
    5: clear versus opaque writing 45
    6: Demetrius on metaphor 59–60
    7: freshness 71
    8: persona 80
    9: cumulative and periodic sentences 89–90
    10: parataxis and hypotaxis 99–100
    11: Demetrius on short sentences for emphasis 108–109
    12: style 115–116
    13: Demetrius on increasing vividness 124–125
    14: texture 136
    15: the levels of style 146
    16: tone 156–157

syllepsis 88–89

symploce 107–108

synecdoche 65–68

tables

    expletives 17

    intensifiers for litotes 25

    phrases for metabasis 30

    question stems for hypophora 35

    transitions of logic 36

    phrases for introducing distinctio 40

    phrases for introducing exemplum 42

    words and phrases for metanoia 44

    methods for constructing similes 51

    methods for constructing metaphors 57

    metaphors and similes turned cliché 71

    epithets 78

    metaphorical epithets 78

    subordinating conjunctions 100

    diagrams for schemes of restatement I 108

    diagrams for schemes of restatement I & II 115

    words used to describe various writing styles 116

    traditional onomatopoeic words 132

    nontraditional onomatopoeic words 132

    two-word consonance 135

    phrases for apophasis 144

texture 136

tone 156–157

transferred epithet 78–80

transitions 35–36

understatement 22–24

vividness 124–125

zeugma 83–84

Instructor's Answer Key

Writing with Clarity and Style

A Guide to
Rhetorical Devices
for
Contemporary Writers

Robert A. Harris

Pyrczak Publishing

P.O. Box 39731 • Los Angeles, CA 90039

Visit us at www.PyrczakExam.com for your examination copy needs.

Instructor's Answer Key to
Writing with Clarity and Style

Chapter 1
Exercise 1.1.1

(a) To install new carpeting, workers must first <u>remove the old carpet</u>, <u>prepare the surface</u>, and then <u>lay down the matting</u>.

(b) Next, the installers need a <u>sharp knife</u> and a <u>sturdy straightedge</u> to cut the new carpet along carefully measured lines.

(c) Several workers are often needed to haul the carpet <u>into the house</u>, <u>up the stairs</u>, and <u>across the room</u>.

Exercise 1.1.2

Answers will vary. Sample answer: The short bushes and the taller trees grew on the slope, hiding the building and blocking the wind.

Exercise 1.1.3

Answers will vary. Sample answers:

(a) I have repeatedly requested but never received an answer to my question.

(b) The puppy ran across the field and under the bleachers.

(c) Applying the primer to the walls and sanding the baseboard near the floor, the painters worked slowly but continuously.

Exercise 1.2.1

(a) After startup, always check the pressure readings, but check the voltage level every hour. *OR* Always check the pressure readings after startup, but every hour check the voltage level. *Comment:* Of the three sentences (original, first, and second chiastic), the first chiastic is probably most effective because it stresses the time elements by putting them at the beginning and the end of the sentence, the positions of most emphasis.

(b) With wood you get easier cutting and nailing, but you avoid termites with steel. *OR* You get easier cutting and nailing with wood, but with steel you avoid termites. *Comment:* In this case, the original parallel construction may be best because it sets up a clear antithesis (contrast) between cutting and nailing and termites, thus emphasizing the idea of avoiding termites. You might let students offer varied opinions about this example and then tell them that they are all correct: The differences are sometimes subtle, and the choice will depend on the writer's desired effect.

Exercise 1.2.2

(a) If the peaches are ripe, turn on the canner. If the apples are ripe, turn on the cider press. *Comment:* Placing the main clause last, as in the parallel construction, appears more effective and emphatic than placing the subordinate clause last. Also, a clearly parallel sequenced pair of if-then sentences is easier to follow logically; and for operating instructions (as we have here), clarity is important.

(b) The buckle should be fitted securely and adjusted regularly. *Comment:* The parallel construction helps avoid a squinting adverb. In the chiastic construction, the reader may think the expression is *fitted securely and regularly*, since *regularly* squints between the two verbs, *fitted* and *adjusted*.

Exercise 1.3.1
   (a) When we jumped out of the airplane, Amy was thrilled, but I was terrified. *OR* When we jumped out of the airplane, the feeling of free falling thrilled Amy but terrified me.
   (b) The proposal should specify a retaining wall that is not only thick but strong as well.

Exercise 1.3.2
Answers will vary. Sample answers follow.
   (a) When I think about what makes a book worth its price, I think more about the content than the length.
   (b) The first lesson on reading forwarded e-mail stories is to learn to distinguish between dubious, exaggerated rumors and reliable, accurate information.

Review Questions
1. P (Remind students that the parallelism can be somewhat loose. Here, *engine of the cruise ship* is paralleled with *plumbing*. Perfect parallelism would require a prepositional phrase as well, such as *plumbing in the rooms*. Similarly, *peacefully quiet* is paralleled with *almost deafeningly loud*. Adding an adverb in front of *peacefully quiet* would make the parallelism more exact.)
   C (If students have difficulty with this one, begin by showing them that the two infinitive phrases *to catch him on the phone* and *to see him in person* are parallel but put at opposite ends of the independent clauses. The same is true of *twenty phone calls* and *an act of Congress*.)
   P (The parallel prepositional phrases and repeated subject verbs *they could* should make this example clear.)
   C (Point out that the *when you* and *they will* are repeated and parallel but at opposite ends of the second clause.)
2. C (Clarify this for students by simplifying it to *arresting is important but painting is crucial*. That may make both the parallelism and the antithesis clearer.)
3. C (Clarify this by asking students to make this one antithetical. An example would be, "She cried and I laughed.")
4. B (Remind students that the parallel elements must be in the same structural position in a sentence, as here, two adjectives. The other options have different structural positions.)

Chapter 2
Exercise 2.1.1
   (a) Today we enjoy many benefits of modern technology, including ballpoint pens, refrigerators, and life-saving antibiotics.
   (b) Natural water storage includes puddles, ponds, lakes, and the oceans.

Exercise 2.2.1
   (a) The fireworks lit the sky with red, blue, green, white, yellow.
   (b) Around the light they saw moths, beetles, mosquitoes, gnats.

Exercise 2.2.2
Answers will vary. Here are some sample answers.
(a) Everywhere she saw the signs of deferred housekeeping: the floors, the furniture, the bedding, the laundry.
(b) She liked to read about far-off lands, about princesses in castles, dancing in the moonlight, dragons guarding their lair, knights battling evil.

Exercise 2.3.1
(a) *Original:* The sparkle of clean water, the peace of silent skies, and the inspiration of giant trees—all these attract me to the forest.
Asyndeton: The sparkle of clean water, the peace of silent skies, the inspiration of giant trees—all these attract me to the forest. (Best. This is the most effective because of the sense of unplanned multiplication of sensory choices and the sense that there may be more choices in the list.)
Polysyndeton: The sparkle of clean water and the peace of silent skies and the inspiration of giant trees—all these attract me to the forest.

(b) *Original:* In that nation, the farmers often have no rakes, hoes, shovels, or pitchforks.
Asyndeton: In that nation, the farmers often have no rakes, hoes, shovels, pitchforks. OR In that nation, the farmers often have no rakes, no hoes, no shovels, no pitchforks. (Best. Asyndeton is the most effective because it implies, in a more powerful way than does the polysyndeton here, that the list may not be complete.)
Polysyndeton: In that nation, the farmers often have no rakes or hoes or shovels or pitchforks.

(c) *Original:* Before beginning the questions, ask the group members how they feel, offer them beverages, and ask if they are comfortable. (Best. This is the most effective because there seem to be these three obvious elements rather than a possibly continuing list of other actions to perform.)
Asyndeton: Before beginning the questions, ask the group members how they feel, offer them beverages, ask if they are comfortable.
Polysyndeton: Before beginning the questions, ask the group members how they feel and offer them beverages and ask if they are comfortable.

Exercise 2.3.2
Answers will vary. Here are some sample answers.
(a) Everywhere she saw the signs of deferred housekeeping, whether the floors or the furniture or the bedding or the laundry. (Comment: In this particular example, the polysyndeton is more effective because of the power of repeated *or*—she seems to be looking at various places around the house.)
(b) She liked to read about far-off lands, about princesses in castles and dancing in the moonlight and dragons guarding their lair and knights battling evil. (Comment: In this particular instance, the asyndeton of Exercise 2.2.2 seems more effective be-

cause it implies that the list is not complete more effectively than does the polysyndeton here.)

Exercise 2.4.1
Answers will vary. Here are some sample answers.
   (a) These early treatments of the disease were crude indeed, but they formed the first steps toward modern control of infection. *OR* Certainly, these early treatments of the disease were crude, but they formed the first steps toward modern control of infection.
   (b) These three plums are still edible, at least. *OR* Remarkably, these three plums are still edible.
   (c) Expletives are, in fact, useful writing tools, but must not be overused. *OR* Clearly, expletives are useful writing tools, but should not be overused.

Exercise 2.4.2
Answers may vary. Here are some recommended answers.
   (a) The food was cold indeed, but we ate it anyway. (Comment: Placing *indeed* directly after *cold* emphasizes the word *cold* rather than the entire sentence.)
   (b) Of course, you could search the Web and hope to find something there. (Comment: Putting the expletive at the beginning of the sentence is a better way to signal emphasis for the entire sentence because the length of the sentence would make an ending expletive arrive too late to cover the entire sentence.)
   (c) This was the result, in fact, of chaos in the newsroom. (Comment: Interrupting the sentence with the expletive forces the phrase *of chaos* to be emphasized, making for a more dramatic sentence.)

Review Questions
1. B (The numbers mount dramatically from low to high.)
2. N, P, N (remind students that *to* is not a conjunction), A
3. Answers will vary. Here are some sample answers.
   (a) He did not take the position lightly. <u>In fact</u>, he was present at every meeting.
   (b) The new coating should extend the corrosion resistance of the pipe by a year, <u>at least</u>.
   (c) <u>In any event</u>, we can expect an increase in attendance at the convention this year.
4. C (*Written* is stressed on the first syllable and *ignored* is stressed on the last.)

Chapter 3
Exercise 3.1.1
   (a) Ironic. The speaker is using exaggeration to criticize exaggeration.
   (b) Not ironic.
   (c) Ironic. We would expect a speaker on punctuality to be on time.

Exercise 3.2.1
Answers will vary. Here are some sample answers.
   (a) Taking over a media conglomerate requires a bit more than loose change.

   (b) Let us now look at some evidence that will show this position has some strength.

   (c) Paying $23,000 for a butterfly pin seems to be on the high side.

Exercise 3.3.1

Answers will vary somewhat. Here are some suggested answers.

   (a) The problem presented by the lost files is not a major issue.

   (b) Unfortunately, the bread at the restaurant is not at all fresh. *OR* less than fresh

   (c) The president announced that he was not optimistic about next quarter's forecast.

Exercise 3.4.1

Answers will vary. Here are some example answers.

   (a) The Tax Simplification Act seems to be millions of pages long.

   (b) She's a successful agent because she knows every single person in the city.

   (c) Not a single second of the game was worth watching.

Review Questions

1. B, D, C, A
2. B
3. B
4. D, A, C, B (Some students might not know that the irony results from the fact that salt is very inexpensive and that no one would imagine a hotel trying to cut back on salt costs.)

Chapter 4

Exercise 4.1.1

Answers will vary. Here are some sample answers.

   (a) Now that we have examined the esthetics of boat design, let us turn to the implications of design and construction on seaworthiness.

   (b) Up to this point, the discussion has focused on the plan and intended results of hunger relief efforts. It remains now to examine the logistics of delivery and distribution of food.

Exercise 4.2.1

Answers will vary. Here are some sample answers.

   (a) Today, children are growing up too fast because they are exposed to adult information (sex, violence, crime, terrorism) at an increasingly young age. There is no time for a carefree childhood. Some defenders of this rapid exposure to adult ideas say that childhood is an outdated concept anyway, and we should not worry about its loss. However, every child should be able to grow emotionally in a secure environment, in order to develop the personality strength and values that will allow him or her to face the pressures of adulthood later on. Childhood should be a treasured, not an outdated concept.

   (b) The modern world is a high-speed, high-pressure place and, fortunately, today's children are growing up with appropriate rapidity. Today's childhood experience is different from that of their grandparents. The hard edge of the modern world is more quickly apparent to children, and they must grow up more quickly to face it. Those troubled by this rapid loss of innocence among the young claim that a carefree childhood is important for personal and emotional growth. This objection, however, looks back to a time that no longer exists: Today's children must grow up fast in order to compete in an ever-faster and higher-pressure environment.

Exercise 4.3.1
Answers will vary. Here are some sample answers.
- (a) Nervous music executives often ask, "How will free music on the Web affect CD music sales?" We can find the answer, I believe, by looking at the power of free samples as a marketing tool. . . .
- (b) The question arises here, Was there evidence of price fixing before the current situation? There have been several claims to that effect, but never any proof. . . .

Review Questions
1. A (You might remind students that the chapter title is Transition.)
2. C, A, B
3. B (Remind students that moving a transition into the sentence makes it milder.)
4. D
5. C

Chapter 5
Exercise 5.1.1
Answers will vary. Here are some sample answers.
- (a) When you take the truck down the mountain, do not drive too fast—that is, do not exceed forty-five miles per hour.
- (b) I'd like to buy an inexpensive car, by which I mean, under $15,000.
- (c) The furniture in that store seems rather old-fashioned. By *old-fashioned*, I mean wooden frames from the sixties and fabrics from the seventies.

Exercise 5.2.1
Answers will vary. Here are some suggested answers.
- (a) This side of the house needs some greenery. For example, hibiscus bushes or Princess trees would work well.
- (b) I remember that town by its odors, such as the wonderful bread aroma that always surrounded Swardlow's Bakery.
- (c) Carbonated beverages have many alternatives, such as tea, coffee, lemonade, and even water.

Exercise 5.3.1
Answers will vary. Here are some sample answers.
- (a) Consumers have been interested in this perfume—this exotic, sensual, and very expensive perfume—in record numbers.
- (b) Last year the winter was unusually cold, a biting cold, a bone-aching cold.
- (c) From the landing, she looked up at the stairs, the stairs that seemed to reach to the sky, and wondered how long the climb would take.

Exercise 5.4.1

Answers may vary somewhat. Here are some suggested answers.

   (a) The team ended the quarter with a very skillful shot, or not so much skillful as lucky.

   (b) At that price we would lose money—or at least make very little.

   (c) The new play equipment will make kids happy, or rather not just kids but everyone who visits the park.

Exercise 5.4.2

Answers will vary. Here are some sample answers.

   (a) If this new tax passes, it will bring investors to financial ruin—or at least to a weakened condition.

   (b) This imported olive oil is very good. No, it is more than very good; it is excellent.

   (c) The inability of investigators to connect seemingly obvious clues because of a "lack of proof" reveals a failure of imagination in their scientific reasoning. Or perhaps it is better to say that the case demonstrates the need for creative thinking skills among investigators in every area.

Review Questions

1. C
2. C
3. B, C, A
4. A
5. C (This item tests Style Check 5.)

Chapter 6

Exercise 6.1.1

Answers may vary slightly.

   (a) The service in this restaurant is as slow as molasses in January.

   (b) Before he could get to work, his ideas dissipated like water on sand.

Exercise 6.2.1

Answers will vary. Here are some sample answers.

   (a) The nutrition book is like a blueprint for a healthy body: It shows you the steps you need to follow in the proper order.

   (b) In a short circuit, a circuit breaker protects the wiring, not a person, just as in an automobile accident, the bumper protects the car and not the passengers. A ground-fault interrupter protects the person during a short, just as the airbag protects the passenger in an accident.

Exercise 6.3.1

Answers will vary. Here are some sample answers.

   (a) The food at the hotel is a magnet for tourists.

(b) We have been assigned an overloaded dump truck of new work.

Exercise 6.3.2

Answers will vary. Here are some sample answers.

(a) The fire hose of information from the Web is a challenge to deal with.

(b) The Web has been called information's fire hose.

(c) On the Web, information is a fire hose coming at you at high speed.

Exercise 6.4.1

Answers will vary depending on the image chosen. Here are some sample answers.

(a) He doors me, girls. He doors me. *OR* He gates me, girls. He gates me.

(b) The little old lady snailed along at ten miles per hour. *OR* caterpillared

Review Questions

1. M (A video is identified as a magic carpet.)

   S (Hair is likened to thorns. The introducing word *like* is present.)

   S (Waves likened to criticism. Introducing word is *as*.)

   N

   M (Time is said to have a voice. Students who have read ahead to Chapter 7 will note that this is an example of personification, a type of metaphor.)

2. C

3. A

4. A (News is compared to a bomb using the introducing word *like*.)

   D (An extravagant metaphor is used: deaf hands.)

   C (Technology is compared to a person or animal with children.)

   B (A comparison supplying conceptual clarification of *falsehood*.)

5. OK

   MM (Hitting with a club will wash a face?)

   OK

   MM (Something airtight can be used as a strainer?)

6. C

Chapter 7

Exercise 7.1.1

(a) the mercury is rising = the temperature is increasing *OR* it's getting hotter

(b) Hollywood = the film industry (You may need to remind students that Hollywood is the name of a neighborhood in Los Angeles.)

Exercise 7.1.2

Answers will vary. Here are some sample answers.

(a) Tomorrow we are going to look at some monkeys and giraffes.

(b) They were being watched by a uniform. *OR* a badge

Exercise 7.2.1

    (a) daily bread = daily food OR a living OR your upkeep

    (b) technology of interruption = telephone OR phone

Exercise 7.2.2

Answers will vary. Here are some sample answers.

    (a) It's time to stretch out on the stuffing and take a nap. (Other terms in place of *stuffing* might be *cotton, springs, padding, comforter*.)

    (b) The workmen spent the day sawing wood and hammering nails. (Note that the activities should be generic rather than specific in order not to imply that only those specific activities were being performed. For example, a general phrase such as *handling pipes and timbers* would be a much clearer indication of general construction than would *installing the plumbing*, which implies a single activity.)

Exercise 7.3.1

Answers will vary. Here are some sample answers.

    (a) smiled OR frowned OR sneered OR laughed OR scowled, etc.

    (b) strolled in OR ambled in OR crept in OR shuffled on over, etc.

    (c) is wandering around OR is lost in the wilderness OR cannot find its way, etc.

    (d) cruel OR heartless OR hateful OR out to get me OR trying to dodge my ball, etc.

Review Questions

1. P (The concept of enlightenment is being personified as a woman.)

   M (Lawyers are being referred to by the metonymy of *suits*, their associated dress.)

   P (The mountain is being personified as a person with likes and dislikes.)

   M (Rain is associated with sorrow, so that *rain in your heart* is a metonymy for sorrow. Similarly, *a warm fireside* is a metonymy for sympathy or recovering joy.)

   M (The stomach is associated with hunger.)

   S (*Sheet metal* is a material-for-thing-made substitution for automobile.)

2. B, C, A

3. C

4. B

5. C (*Nuts and bolts* is worn out.)

   C (*Ladder of success* is worn out.)

   F (*Spice rack* is reasonably fresh.)

   C (*Bite the bullet* is worn out.)

   F (The personification of problems as riders and walkers is reasonably fresh.)

   F (*A dung beetle's treasure*, a ball of dung, is a reasonably fresh image.)

Chapter 8
Exercise 8.1.1
Answers will vary somewhat. Here are some sample answers.
- (a) This memo came from the boss. That makes these new policies like the Ten Commandments, engraved in stone.
- (b) When he saw the bill, he gave the table a shake like that from the 1994 Northridge earthquake.

Exercise 8.2.1
Answers will vary somewhat. Here are some sample answers.
- (a) We need a fund manager with the touch of Midas.
- (b) Many magazines today splash a Helen of Troy on the cover to increase sales.

Exercise 8.3.1
Answers will vary somewhat. Here are some sample answers.
- (a) Next week I'm going to the dentist. O my teeth! How I feel for you!
- (b) The winter deepened and the snows came. Ah snow! How I love you!

Exercise 8.4.1
Answers will be widely varied. Here are some example answers.
- (a) *The Vertigo Thickens* was a rather leafy motion picture, with pieces of the plot branching off in all directions.
- (b) A good agent will never ask you to sign such a smoggy contract.

Review Questions
1. C (The writer addresses the trees.)
   B (Mother Theresa is an eponym standing for a charitable, caring person.)
   D (Slithering normally refers to snakes, not tires.)
   A (The writer alludes to a famous historical event: climbing Everest.)
2. C, A, D, B
3. D (*Tea-drinking road* is a personification, but more unusual than, say, *lazy road*.)
4. B (Several synonymous expressions will clarify the meaning.)
5. B (Persona is the reader's view of the writer.)

Chapter 9
Exercise 9.1.1
- (a) The workman drilled into the base rock and through the rock wall.
- (b) The people voted for more limits on government and more services, too.

Exercise 9.2.1
- (a) The spotlight slipped from the mounting and crashed to the floor.

(b) To create the wallpaper, the artist copied the shapes of diatoms, colored the shapes with bright paints, and then assembled the pictures randomly.

Exercise 9.3.1
  (a) The digital copier reduces the need for printed originals; e-mail, the need for hard-copy memos; and the Web, the need for printed articles.
  (b) Heraclitus argued that you cannot step into the same river twice; Zeno, that you will never arrive at the river in the first place.

Exercise 9.4.1
  (a) The governor left the news conference, and then the reporter.
  (b) The intended benefits of the bill were considered, but not the unintended costs.

Exercise 9.5.1
  (a) Purifying their own water, processing their own waste, and generating their own electricity, the new cruise ships are designed to be like cities.
  (b) The roadway, the bridge, and the hotel are features made of stone.

Exercise 9.6.1
  (a) When daylight saving time ends, change your clocks, your smoke alarm batteries, and your mind about sleeping late.
  (b) He liked the coffee shop in the bookstore because in one place he could feed his mind and his stomach.

Review Questions
1. B, D, C, A
2. S, S, Z
3. P, C, C, P
4. C

Chapter 10
Exercise 10.1.1
  (a) Chocolate I like and chocolate I will eat.
  (b) The film rights to the novel, because of an error in the contract, were lost.

Exercise 10.2.1
  (a) She sang with a voice unrestrained.
  (b) These are valuable experiments and carefully performed.
  (c) Mr. Perkins required a dangerous operation but necessary.

Exercise 10.3.1
  (a) That afternoon, Mom showed the kids a new game: <u>raking leaves</u>.

(b) The red manual, <u>an outline of steps to take in an emergency</u>, should be kept within easy reach.

(c) <u>A product of robotic manufacturing</u>, the fan had been made at night in the dark after the plant workers had gone home.

Exercise 10.3.2
Answers will vary. Here are some sample answers.

(a) Now an old rusting hulk, the tractor sat unused at the edge of the farm.

(b) I would like to speak to Mr. Granger, the president of the company, about this radio.

(c) The library needs one last piece of furniture, a rolltop desk.

Exercise 10.4.1
Answers will vary somewhat. Here are some suggested answers.

(a) The use of edge enhancement (an image-sharpening process) made the photographs much clearer.

(b) Swimmers should be careful—parents please watch your children—to avoid the area where the jellyfish are located.

(c) Applying the factory-recommended torque (check the manual) is essential to prevent either a loose fitting or a broken bolt.

Style Check Exercise 10.1
Answers will vary. Here are some sample answers.

(a) Because the reporters were curious about the paint spill, they asked about its source.

(b) When one of the generators broke down, the cruise ship lost half its power. *OR* The cruise ship lost half its power after one of the generators broke down.

(c) Freeways have been built for decades now, while the architecture of overpasses has changed little. *OR* Even though freeways have been built for decades now, the architecture of overpasses has changed little.

Style Check Exercise 10.2
Answers will vary. Here are some sample answers.

(a) The divers swam to the coral reef, and they photographed the larger formations. [Note: omitting *they* would be acceptable, creating a zeugmatic construction.]

(b) George I was king of England, but he spoke German, not English.

(c) Research and development are important, for new products are our future.

Review Questions
1. C, B, A
2. A, N, A
3. P, P, H, H
4. D
5. B

Chapter 11
Exercise 11.1.1
   (a) Their need to feel trendy resulted in a house filled with designer furniture, designer curtains, designer clothes, and even designer soap.
   (b) We will search in the hills, we will search among the rocks, we will search in the underbrush, we will search over the whole area. And we will find the lost child.

Exercise 11.2.1
   (a) When the boy arrived home from school, his shoes were wet, his clothes were wet, and his books were wet.
   (b) The international construction project required workers from many countries and financing from many countries.

Exercise 11.3.1
   (a) The bill is generated electronically, and the bill can be paid electronically.
   (b) Place the outline at the beginning of each chapter, and place the recap at the end of each chapter.

Review Questions
1. C, A, B
2. B
3. A
4. B, C, A
5. B, A, C

Chapter 12
Exercise 12.1.1
   (a) Next weekend we will drive to Lava Beds National Monument to explore the caves. The caves are actually very interesting old lava tubes.
   (b) The vast quantities of mineral nodules on the ocean floor are only one reminder of the value of sea mining; sea mining is an opportunity yet unexploited in the quest for industrial metals.

Exercise 12.2.1
   (a) Margarita fed the goldfish every day with the new pellets brought from Japan. The goldfish began to turn a brighter orange after a few weeks.
   (b) Cleaning the years of yellowing varnish from the painting revealed that the men were sword fighting in the daytime, not at night. The daytime explained why the men were squinting.

Exercise 12.3.1
   (a) Invasion they may threaten, but we will resist invasion.
   (b) Real gold may have been what you wanted, but what you bought is only fool's gold.

Review Questions

1. C (*Broken* is repeated at the beginning of the first main clause and the end of the second main clause.)

   A (*Glassy rod* ends the first sentence and begins the next.)

   B (*Words* is pulled out of the first sentence and repeated at the beginning of the next.)

2. B (Style Check 12 on Style discusses the distinction.)

3. B (Conduplicatio allows the writer to repeat a key word from the previous sentence.)

4. B (The word *habits* ends one clause and begins another. This is a good example to explain why the repetition is said to be at *or near* the beginning of the subsequent clause or sentence. Here, the word *because* actually comes first.)

   C (The key word *bug* is repeated at the beginning of the second sentence.)

   A (*To be* is present at the beginning and end of the expression.)

5. B (A key word is pulled out and begins the subsequent sentence.)

   C (The same word or words are present at the beginning and the end.)

   A (The same word that ends one clause or sentence begins another.)

Chapter 13

Exercise 13.1.1

Expect some variation in punctuation and wording. Here are some typical answers.

(a) The bite of a leech is completely painless—yes, completely painless—because the leech produces an anesthetic that numbs the area it bites.

(b) Toll road charges now increase—naturally there is never a decrease—toll road charges now increase during busier times of the day.

Exercise 13.2.1

Students may choose either two or three instances of the underlined word. Here are some recommended answers.

(a) The faded, faded watercolor painting was still valuable because of its pale beauty.

(b) The speaker realized his need for improvement when he looked up from his notes and saw yawns, yawns, yawns.

Exercise 13.3.1

(a) There was mutual benefit: The company helped Jones and Jones helped the company.

(b) Some advertisements are as memorable as the product: The ad reminds us of the product and the product reminds us of the ad.

Exercise 13.4.1

Answers will vary. Here are some example answers.

(a) The cloth felt smooth and soft, sleek and velvety, satiny and plush.

(b) The mountain climbers carried the heavy supplies, lugging the weighty burdens themselves.

Review Questions

1. D (Three synonymous expressions.)

   B (Repetition of one word.)

   A (Repetition of *first around the edges* with intervening words.)

   C (Reversal of amusement/restaurant idea.)

2. B (The colors [*orange, white, black, gray*] and the sounds [*spitting, sparking*] and the imagery of juices dripping make this much more vivid than the other choices.)

3. D (Synonyms allow the writer to express more aspects or nuances of an idea than simply repeating the same words. Synonyms have similar meanings to each other rather than exactly the same meaning as each other. This slight difference is a powerful tool for enriching a description or the presentation of an idea.)

4. C (Repetition of *time is passing* with intervening words.)

   D (Repetition of one word.)

   A (Reversal of beliefs and actions.)

   B (A string of synonymous expressions.)

5. A (Repetition of *words* with intervening expletive.)

   C (Reversal of A and B.)

   B (Repetition of one word.)

   D (Several synonymous expressions.)

Chapter 14

Exercise 14.1.1

Answers will vary. Here are some suggested answers.

   (a) Come walk the length of our beautiful beach. *OR* You won't believe our sensational sand! *OR* Have we got a carefree coastline just for you!

   (b) We remember, every holiday, the solitary souls who have no family to come to dinner. *OR* It's the living lonely we most feel compassion for in this season of celebration.

Exercise 14.2.1

Answers will vary. Here are some sample answers.

   (a) The screeches, shrieks, and growls we heard in the forest frightened us.

   (b) The sizzling steak smelled wonderful.

Exercise 14.3.1

Answers will vary. Here are some sample answers.

   (a) From the window, she wondered how much the traffic cop was <u>paid</u> to stand in the <u>rain</u>.

   (b) He paid the <u>bill</u> with a <u>grin</u> and left a <u>fitting tip</u>, too.

Exercise 14.4.1

Answers will vary. Here are some sample answers.

   (a) The cowhands <u>led</u> the cattle in, <u>applied</u> the <u>brand</u>, and <u>rode</u> back for another <u>herd</u>.

   (b) The gambler could not <u>shake</u> his bad <u>luck</u>.

Review Questions

1. B (*Chomp* and *crunchy* are onomatopoeic.)

 D (*Brightest, float,* and *street* produce consonance.)

 C (*Line, kite,* and *high* produce assonance.)

 A (*Blue-bladed* alliterates.)

2. C, A, B, D

3. B

4. B

5. C

Chapter 15

Exercise 15.1.1

Answers may vary somewhat.

 (a) Is the gore film, with its lurid chemical blood and wiggly silicone guts, the best we can expect from the film industry?

 (b) Should the senator be impeached for acting in good faith, though in error?

Exercise 15.2.1

Answers may vary somewhat.

 (a) I cannot say who was the most content: the child in the swing, the woman on the porch, or the man in the garden.

 (b) I wonder whether those who did not vote wish now they had.

Exercise 15.3.1

Answers may vary somewhat.

 (a) I don't need to remind you to bring warm clothing to the winter resort in the mountains.

 (b) It need not be mentioned that this new computer system is more fun than the one we use now.

Exercise 15.4.1

Answers may vary somewhat.

 (a) The kids were unusually noisy, the classroom felt like an oven, and the playground—I tell you my day was a nightmare.

 (b) The buffet has crab legs, venison, prime rib, salmon, pork chops—I want it all.

Review Questions

1. D, C, A, B

2. C (Apophasis "passes over" something in the process of mentioning it.)

 A (Rhetorical question is not answered.)

 D (Anacoluthon leaves the first sentence unfinished.)

 B (Aporia expresses doubt or ignorance.)

3. B

4. B

5. C (A research paper is most likely to be formal, while an e-mail to a friend will most likely be informal. An essay revealing one's personality to a stranger will most likely be semiformal.)

Chapter 16

Exercise 16.1.1
- (a) T
- (b) T
- (c) R
- (d) T
- (e) T
- (f) R
- (g) T
- (h) R
- (i) T
- (j) R

Exercise 16.1.2
Answers will vary. Here are some sample answers.
- (a) Automobile insurance fraud has increased in recent years, largely because of criminals who stage planned accidents.
- (b) Judging by how rarely meteorologists can accurately predict whether we will see rain, snow, or sun a week from today, I would say the term *weather forecast* is a contradiction in terms.

Exercise 16.2.1
Answers will vary somewhat. Here are example answers.
- (a) *Armorgeddon* puns on the words *armor* and *Armageddon* by combining the two words into one new one (a neologism).
- (b) *Stumble in the spring* causes the reader to reanalyze *trip in the fall* and see the punning meanings of *trip* (a catch of the foot) and *fall* (to drop suddenly), in addition to their original meanings of *journey* and *autumn season*.
- (c) The phrase *goes to waist* suggests the more common phrase *goes to waste*.

Exercise 16.2.2
Answers will be individual. Here are some example answers.
- (a) Your reply seems to be sailing around the point, when I wish it would dock. (Pun on the point of an argument and a point of land.)
- (b) We serve a decent fare at a fair price. If you don't like it, fare thee well; take your fair friend, pay your fare and bus away.

Exercise 16.3.1

Answers will vary. Here are some sample answers.

    (a) How can we cattle prod this case and get it moving through the court?

    (b) She walked into the bake without looking back at the car. *OR* They stumbled through the bake toward the oasis.

Review Questions

1. B (*Bear* and *bare* are homonyms but not homographs.)

   C (The adverb *slowly* is used as a noun.)

   A (Students who enjoy crying over books and films will relate to this one.)

2. A

3. D

4. D

5. C (This question tests Style Check 16.)

A Note on the Appendices

For Appendices A through E, where students are asked to revise texts and add rhetorical devices, there are three possible degrees of guidance you may wish to consider. The first level is no guidance at all. The students have the paragraphs, the example texts, and the devices in the book, and must use their own creativity and knowledge to add devices.

The second level is to require a list of devices, such as one metaphor, one expletive, and one conduplicatio. (You may want to go beyond the minimums suggested in the exercises and require more than three devices for each text.)

The third level of guidance is to suggest particular devices for specific sentences. For example, "In sentence one, add an appositive; in sentence three, use onomatopoeia; in sentence four, add parallelism to the ideas." Adding some guidance will help students practice a variety of devices. (When the appendix exercises were tested, one student displayed a tremendous fondness for alliteration over most other devices.)

Appendix A

Exercise A.1

Student paragraphs will vary widely. Here is a sample paragraph.

At its regular meeting last night, the City Council proposed to install new, electronic parking meters in the downtown area. These meters, unlike the ones in use now, will "zero out"—they will lose their memory, forget anyone ever paid them, register zero on the dial[1]—the moment a car leaves the spot, regardless of the time otherwise left on the meter.

As a result, there will be no more "free time," which really means time already paid for by someone else.[2] For many downtown drivers, a few free minutes smiling from a parking meter[3] was the only bright moment in a depressingly dreary[4] parking experience.[5]

The council members say this change will produce additional revenue. However, no specific dollar figures were trotted out and paraded around,[6] leaving us to doubt that any such figures exist.[7] After all, the new meters are expensive. Recovering their cost will take a long time, leaving a long time[8] before the city will hear the chink, chink[9] of net revenue.

This proposal makes neither dollars nor sense.[10] We hope the city will cash out of it.[11]

1. Amplification, presented as scesis onomaton, and in personified fashion
2. Distinctio, to clarify the real meaning of "free time"
3. Personification
4. Alliteration
5. Metaphor (bright and dreary, suggesting weather)
6. Metaphor, seeing dollars as horses
7. Aporia
8. Anadiplosis
9. Onomatopoeia
10. Pun
11. Pun, based on the figurative and literal meanings of *cash out*

Appendix B
Exercise B.1
Student paragraphs will vary widely. Here is a sample paragraph.

To: All Association Managers
From: Pat Olley, VP Customer Relations
Re: Guaranteed Contractors

According to recent surveys, a major concern of both our homeowners association board members and the residents of our associations is that of finding a reliable contractor to do work (such as painting, landscaping, or plumbing)[1] for them individually. Many members appear to fear that contractors all too often will either overcharge them or perform work of questionable quality.[2] Whether or not that reflects reality,[3] it is a common perception.

To address this concern, Triangle Property Management has developed a list of contractors who have proven reliable in their services in the past, have agreed to guarantee their work, and will settle all disputes through arbitration with a TPM associate.[4]

Please inform your board members at their next meeting of this new list and that, with their approval, we will be happy to distribute this new list.[5] The last thing we want is unhappy residents, anxious and uncertain,[6] when we can ride to the rescue[7] and help solve their dilemma.

1. Parenthesis, containing an exemplum, to clarify the kinds of work under consideration. The parenthesis saves time and space (another sentence is not needed).
2. Parallelism for easier reading and understanding of the two concerns.

3. Aporia, injecting a bit of doubt in order to distance the writer from the claim. Perhaps the writer believes that the perception is exaggerated.
4. Parallelism, to show the three components of the program all together. The construction also involves diazeugma, where the three verb phrases are linked to the single relative pronoun *who*.
5. Epistrophe, repeating *new list* at the end of clauses, to fix the concept in the mind of the reader. In other words, the memo announces a new program, which is made tangible in the form of a new list.
6. Anastrophe, putting the adjectives *anxious and uncertain* behind the noun *residents* in order to emphasize the adjectives over the noun.
7. Metaphor. While not very original, the metaphor does add some vividness and concrete imagery to the discussion of the abstract program.

Appendix C

Exercise C.1

Student paragraphs will vary widely. Here is a sample paragraph.

Jennifer is an 18-year-old freshman at a first-rank private university, the same school her father attended.[1] Her father is now divorced and has put his hopes of success in his daughter. He wants her to drive down the same career road[2] and become a medical doctor. He has announced that he will not permit her to fail.

Jennifer sought the social worker's help because she has been suffering from anxiety, insomnia, self-doubt, nightmares (when she does sleep), and panic attacks.[3] Even though she earned A's in high school, she has found the university to be substantially more challenging. Where she saw high school as a guaranteed success, she fears that college will be an inevitable failure.[4] She feels conflicted because her father wants her to be a doctor, even though she would like to study art or architecture.

I reassured her that she was not alone in her concerns. I told her there were, in fact,[5] many possible solutions. I urged her to have a talk with her father about her own aspirations. I also put her in contact with the Study Skills Center for help with time management. She appeared relieved—relieved to the point of happy tears—[6]at the end of our session.

1. Appositive, for smoothness, clarity, and emphasis
2. Metaphor
3. The list reorganized into climactic order for better understanding of the severity of each symptom
4. Anthitheis and parallelism, contrasting *guaranteed success* with *inevitable failure*, to help reveal the source of Jennifer's fear and stress
5. Expletive to emphasize the *many possible solutions*
6. Amplification, parenthesis, and oxymoron

22

Appendix D

Exercise D.1

Student paragraphs will vary widely. Here is a sample paragraph.

I am applying to your graduate program in forensic science because I have always been attracted to the *how* of crime.[1] As a child, I read the Sherlock Holmes stories; in high school I devoured[2] murder mysteries; and in college, I have learned from books about arson investigation, crime-scene searching, and autopsies.[3] I love a challenge, a puzzle,[4] and I look forward to a career solving challenging crimes.

By majoring in chemistry, I have laid the bricks of a solid foundation[5] for studies about toxicology and drug analysis, and I have taken a course in human anatomy to prepare me for further study relating to the joints and disjoints of the body.[6] Many of my courses have emphasized the scientific method.

For the past two years, I have had a part-time job at a pharmacy. There, I have learned as much as possible about the effects of various medicines, learned how legal medicines are sometimes abused, and even learned a little about poisoning, all from a practical point of view.[7]

I believe my academic preparation and my lifelong interest in forensic science will enable me to succeed in your program and to become a valuable asset to solving crimes.

1. Anthimeria, using *how* as a noun. The use of *how* focuses the idea on the problem-solving aspect of a criminal investigation.

2. Metaphor, much more lively than the original's *read*.

3. Parallelism (*I read, I devoured, I learned*) to clarify the sequencing and to show a change, through the changing verbs, in the student's attitude toward the material.

4. Scesis onomaton, presented in the form of an appositive. The addition of another term helps define the idea more clearly.

5. Metaphor, to provide some visual texture to the sentence.

6. Synecdoche, with *joints* standing for the entire anatomy and *disjoints* standing for whatever traumas are wreaked on human bodies during the course of crime.

7. Diazeugma with parallelism and anaphora. The anaphora repeats *learned* to emphasize that the student has gained knowledge in all of these areas.

Appendix E

Exercise E.1

Student paragraphs will vary widely. Here is a sample paragraph.

A family drove out to the desert, where they came upon an area with petrified wood. Nature had painted many of the rocks beautifully,[1] showing patches of brown and red and yellow and black.[2]

"Pick one to take home for a souvenir," said the father.

"Which should I choose?" his daughter asked, dazzled by the many possibilities.

"The best alternative cannot be selected until you identify, rank, and weight the preferred criteria in your decision-modeling process," her father replied.

"Just choose the prettiest one that's nearby, honey," said her mother, while giving her husband a look.

"I want a heavy one," their son offered, "so I can <u>smash</u>[3] bugs." Soon the boy found a suitable <u>bug-crunching</u>[4] rock, <u>heavy but ugly</u>.[5]

"What about you, dear?" asked the girl's mother.

"Well," the girl replied, "these rocks are all pretty, but I'd really rather have an ice cream cone."

"<u>This is *your* DNA</u>,[6] you know," said the woman to her husband.

The moral: <u>A choice selects from among the stated alternatives; a wise choice selects from its own alternatives.</u>[7]

1. Personification (*Nature*) and metaphor (*painted*)
2. Polysyndeton
3. Onomatopoeia
4. Onomatopoeia
5. Anastrophe
6. Synecdoche
7. Epistrophe, antithesis, and parallelism. Note also the presence of metonymic personification (*a choice selects*), where *choice* is a metonymy for the chooser.